CONTENTS

Introduction

I encountered Slenderman personally in the late fall of 2010.

Like I occasionally do, I was perusing some of the paranormal sections of internet image boards. As a writer of the unexplained I have found many interesting modern legends and stories in these dark corners of the internet. And as I read what was to be my first encounter with the fictional Slenderman mythos, the hair began to sand up on the back of my neck. The part of the legend that struck me most was the eternal stalking nature of the tall man. That once you see him as a child he would follow you till the day you die. He will be forever stalking you from the shadowy places at the periphery of your vision. This entity will be waiting for you with an unceasing desire for your soul, watching with undead eyes that never blink or lose their focus.

After I read the article I had the distinct feeling that I was being watched. Something...other....was watching me. It was not the odd tingle when you know someone is watching you behind your back. It was stronger than that. It was as if I was being keenly observed by a predator.

So as I usually do when feeling oppressed by a real or imagined threat I said a prayer commanding any entity involved to leave. Within a few minutes the feeling left.

But that odd acute feeling left an impression on me. I had not had such a strong reaction for many, many years.

I have had multiple experiences with demonic and malevolent entities since the early 1980s. From 1984 onwards I have been involved with helping counsel people who have demonic oppression and performing the rite of exorcism. As a seminary trained exorcist I have ministered to a myriad of individuals who have been harassed physically and emotionally by (usually) unseen evil. Many times these encounters turn out to be undiagnosed or untreated psychological disorders. But every so often I have come across the real thing. After a while, you get used to it, a kind of desensitization to the shock and fear associated with a confrontation with tangible evil. Demonic entities are often miserable and almost pitiable creatures. However, every once in a while you would come across a strong creature that would have a hold over an individual, family or residence. But I had not felt that odd creepy feeling like I did in the fall of 2010 for a long time.

I instinctually knew there was something to this Slenderman mythos. And a few weeks later I received an email asking for help with a demonic oppression. I receive a few of these a week, and after going over the specifics I noticed that the entity described had manifest itself as a tall thin man dressed in black. It had thin limbs that were abnormally long that had reached out from the foot of the victims bed. She claimed she had seen this in dreams and late night encounters since a child. As I read the narrative, I had to stop and gather my senses, for the entity had an unmistakable resemblance to Slenderman. It was then it hit me, I had heard many similar descriptions of malevolent entites like this described before. So I waded through many old cases and I was astonished at what I had found. Since I had begun my ministry in the field of "power encounter" with malicious entities I had been hearing of stories of the tall thin man who lives in the shadows. Was this Slenderman a real entity? I had a massive amount of personal encounters with an diabolical being that mirrored Slenderman to a tee. From hauntings to supposed alien abductions, it seemed the tall thin man was a prevalent in many individuals experiences with unexplainable phenomenon.

As I have done more research, I have found that the Slenderman mythos goes far beyond internet fiction. Indeed it has been a multi cultural phenomenon for thousands of years.

In this book we shall explore the history of the fictional Slenderman and its connection to many millennia's worth of myth and legend. We shall then examine many personal encounters with the entity that takes the Slenderman form and how to respond to such encounters if you should ever have them.

The Internet Myth

Officially, Slenderman was created through an internet contest when the readers of the "Something Awful" forums were asked to create a fictional paranormal entity in a thread named "Create Paranormal Images".

The scheme was to create eerie images and use them to trick people on paranormal forums into thinking they were genuine. Users started Photoshopping images by adding fake ghosts and other bizarre figures, usually accompanied by a fake back story to make them seem authentic.

On May 1, 2009 a forum user who was named "Gerogerigegege" started the challenge by announcing on the new thread:
"Creating paranormal images has been a hobby of mine for quite some time. Occasionally, I stumble upon odd web sites showcasing strange photos, and I always wondered if it were possible to get one of my own chops in a book, documentary, or web site just by casually leaking it out into the web --

whether they'd be supplements to bogus stories or not.

So, let's make a sh**load?

Pro-tip 1: Before I export, I like to open my Levels panel, and slide my blacks and whites inward to lose true whites and true blacks. (Makes it look more legit, no?)
Pro-tip 2: Try exporting your image in a very low JPG quality at first. See if it works with the image, as well as hide minor flaws. After all, it can "add to the effect."

You don't have to post your source images, unless you want to of course."
Gerogerigegege then added the following photoshop image of his own creation:

 It is called "Mincy".

What followed was a storm of photoshopped images with horrifying stories. Some of the images were quite professional, and many pf the stories were chilling. However, two photos with only small captions for the pictures descriptions mesmerized the forum community. On June 10th 2009 at 2:07PM an artist named Victor Surge posted the first pictures of Slenderman, Here are the photos and the accompanying captions:

"we didn't want to go, we didn't want to kill them, but its persistent silence and outstretched arms horrified and comforted us at the same time..."
1983, photographer unknown, presumed dead.

"One of two recovered photographs from the Stirling City Library blaze. Notable for being taken the day which fourteen children vanished and for what is referred to as "The Slender Man". Deformities cited as film defects by officials. Fire at library occurred one week later. Actual photograph confiscated as evidence."

1986, photographer: Mary Thomas, missing since June 13th, 1986

The next day June 11th, 2009 at 4:55PM Surge followed up with another photo and a supposed police report from 1955 that was covered in blood and insane scribbling which indicates an encounter with Slenderman.

The report is made out by Officer D.W. Dixon at 6:06PM on December 1, 1955. A miscellaneous incident in front of the Empire Theatre was reported to the police by a woman named J.F. Blake . Scribbled across the report are the words: *"Slenderman, Slenderman, kill us already, kill us, kill, kill, kill"* and next to the location on the report is the date 6/15/97 and the circled statement

"Wilksis Place" and "Same place, same, same, same, same"

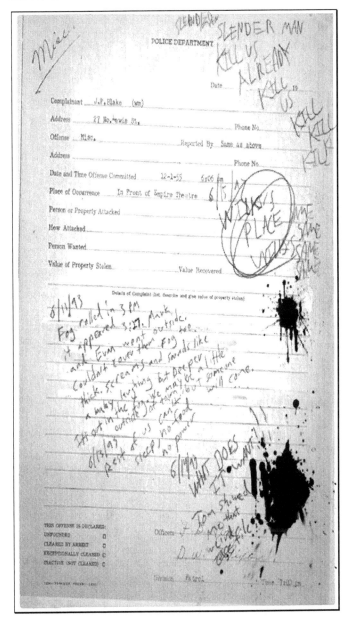

Sprawled across the bottom half of the page is the description of an incident that happened the night of 6/11/93:

"*Fog rolled in 3pm it appeared 3:27. Mark and Evan went outside. Couldn't cover them fog too thick. Screams and sounds like a baby laughing but deeper. It's out in the fog. We may be a little outside of town but someone will come.*"

The next entry is on 6/14/93, which reads,

"*WHAT DOES IT WANT!!! Tom showed me that weird file.*"

Victor Surge further added to the myth by posting more creative material the next day, June 12th 2009. These photos and drawings detailed the eerie disappearance of a young boy the day after his birthday party.

Come to a Dinosaur Party
to celebrate Jake's Birthday!

Saturday, May 18th

2:00 pm to 4:00 pm

1545 North Ridge View Lane

regrets to Carla 509. 877.1992

Look between the trees in this next photo of the
birthday party itself...

Evidently, Slenderman took its victim not soon afterward.

The Daily W

Tuesday, May 21st, 2004

Local Boy Disappears

Wichita - A missing 8-year-old boy, Jake Greenwood of Wichita, Kansas, has his neighborhood in an uproar. The boy went missing from his backyard around approximately 5:20 PM on Sunday the 19th of May. His mother reported seeing him playing near the trees of his backyard prior to his disappearance and noticed nothing suspicious.

School officials state that in the weeks leading up to his disappearance, that he had been unitable at school and at home, often complaining of a tall, very thin man in all black. Police declined to comment at this time.

Rem
foll
imp

The
that
rela
the
beh
of a
exp
in li
its

This story added to the mythology in that Slenderman was now connected directly to trees and tree limbs. The second supposed picture by 7 year old Jake shows the tree (or is it Slenderman himself) reaching out to him with limbs. Soon Slenderman was envisioned as having tendril arms sprouting from his back with which he ensnared his victims. This connection with trees and wooded areas was further established in Surge's next update on June 13, 2009.

This photo was captioned, "Steinmen Woods" and the following story was included with the photo: *"Both subjects were hunting in the Steinmen woods four hours before sundown. Surviving subject states*

*that while hunting both men grew uneasy as fog
levels rapidly increased. A constant murmuring
sound accompanied by a low hum eventually
became apparent to the two men an hour after the
fog increased. An object falling out of tree stuck one
of the men in the left shoulder causing him to
discharge his weapon. Object said to be the body of
a man of unknown age. It was very precisely
dissected, with major internal organs still contained
within the rib cage in what looked to be clear bags.
Surviving subject placed organ bag within
backpack. Attack followed several minutes later
after a "low children's laugh, like a giggle".
Surviving subject ran until he reached his vehicle.
Subject then drove to assumed safety.*

*Backpack destroyed.
Surviving subject is classified as a B7 witness. B7
witness to be placed in quarantine "Blind Box" until
resolution."*

Another photo and short description was included
with this one. It also detailed a woodland encounter
with Slenderman which led to death in 2007:

The description reads:

*"2007:Investigation team discovered twenty-two bodies of both genders and various ages impaled on broken tree branches in a radiating circle pattern with chest mutilation as often noted with Slender Man. Upon confirmation, lead investigator ********* called for an immediate evacuation of investigation team at 1700 hours. Bodies first discovered at 1100 hours. Deadline for safe evacuation of team with only viewed physical evidence of Slender Man approximately 1730. Lost contact of team at 1725. Safety procedures fell well within established protocols. Reason for abnormality is unknown. Second team recovered camera equipment one week later. Slender Man*

safety procedures require this incident's physical photographic evidence to be disposed of by no later than 10/20.

I honestly don't get what half this poo poo means. I'm done with this Slender Man stuff. It's starting to make me uneasy. It's like reading the GBS ghost story threads before I go to bed. Why do I have to look at this stuff while it's super late?

Luckily, my friend is coming over."

Slenderman as a haunting entity associated with residences was the next step for the myth. Victor posted this photo and description on the same day, June 13, 2009:

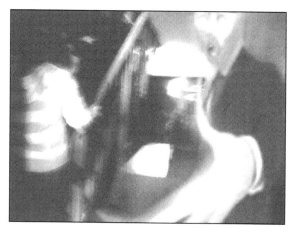

The caption reads: "*My friend is herejus camein barely made up staairs got pictur locked door but it s right there inthe hall*
dont look at its pictures it dosent want to be known about dont loo"

Between these last posts, Slenderman was the talk of the forum thread, and the myth began to seep out into various image boards across the internet. Surge's modified photos and descriptions spread from website to website as the internet generation seemed both captivated and haunted by this malicious entity.

Soon discussion between the forum posters and Surge led to some modifications of the Slenderman image. One poster named "Thoreau-Up" wrote, "*I think the Slender Man's tentacles need to be a little less obvious. It seems a lot less freakier if you can see them so clearly.*" Another poster named "WoodrowSkillson" concurred, adding "*I agree, its better when you don't notice them at first, and only later you realize just how alien the Sender Man is.*"

Surge replied, "*Yeah, I wanted the last set of images to be more obvious, since the people taking the pictures kinda knew what they dealing with and therefore could get better shots (before it wiped them out), and I kinda wanted to bring it to a close. I'm glad everyone enjoyed it, although initially it hadn't been my intent to do more past the first picture post. What essentially inspired me was stuff like "The Rake", since that pretty much terrified me. Having an unearthly creature, such as a skinwalker or something, stalking you has always been much scarier than ghosts in my opinion.*

As for image assets, I used a lot. I have folder with about seventy different things in it."

A poster named "Splash Damage" asked Surge where he came up with the idea of Slenderman; was it original or from another source. Surge answered, "*The Slender Man as an idea was made-up off the top of my head, although the concept is based on a number of things that scare me. The name I thought up on the fly when I wrote that first bit. The asset I used for a couple of the pictures was the creepy tall guy from Phantasm, which sadly I have not seen, and the others various guys in suits. All of the things that aren't the torso and legs, like the tentacles and Slender Man's face, were painted from scratch however."*

After this Victor Surge sat back and let others play with his creation. Soon Slenderman became a popular internet Meme and a subject of much discussion in every creative avenue of the internet. Speculative fiction was created with various associations of Slenderman to past historical boogeymen and legends.

Marble Hornets

(http://marblehornets.wikidot.com/start)

On June 20, 2009 an ARG (Alternative Reality Game) called "Marble Hornets" was created using the newly created Slenderman mythos as the centerpiece of the game.

According to the Slenderman Wiki, and ARGs are *"interactive storytelling devices that make use of real-world interaction, devices, and media to add realism and help tell a story, which may be altered by 'participant' action..*

In the Slenderman universe, videomakers use their series' YouTube channels as a way for interaction. These series are referred to as ARGs. The use of Twitter accounts, mail, and Ustream is also included in Slenderman ARGs.

Actions within the ARG narrative are referred to as IG, or In Game. Following the popularity of MarbleHornets, many Slenderblogs were created- that is, blog-based ARGs or narratives."

According to the Slenderman wikia, Marble Hornets gains its name from a film project by a man named Alex who disappears while attempting to document Slenderman stalking him.

"The early entries in the series are clips from the filming tapes used in creating the Marble Hornets film. Alex ended the project due to seeing Slenderman (known in MH as The Operator) frequently, and handed the tapes over to his friend and MH narrator Jay. Alex told Jay to burn the tapes, but, being a good friend, Jay did not and

instead posted them on Youtube. Alex disappeared afterwards.

Early entries consisted of tapes from the Marble Hornets film and of those taken by Alex who obsessively recorded himself in order to capture Slenderman stalking him. Eventually, the entries turn to videos taken by Jay, cataloguing his efforts to discover Alex's whereabouts and unravel the mystery surrounding The Operator.

Over time, Jay follows leads to old buildings, former homes, etc, but generally finds little to nothing. He begins to encounter two figures-Masky, the video series' Proxy, and The Operator itself, who seemingly work together to antagonize Jay and separate him from Alex.

Some videos receive cryptic responses from a separate Youtube channel called totheark, which makes threats, predictions, and statements concerning the on goings of the entries as they progress.[1]"

---

[1] http://theslenderman.wikia.com/wiki/MarbleHornets last accessed 5/17/2012

Marble Hornets is still ongoing and even has an entry on the Internet Movie Database. Since its inception many other ARGs and interactive blogs have been created in the Slenderman mythos. At the time of this writing (May 2012), there are 738,000 results when searching for Slenderman on Google.

The Slenderman Mythos has become an internet phenomenon.

Mythos Growth

With the popularity of the Slenderman mythos growing by leaps and bounds across the Internet, the expansion of the mythos by the various creative community was a natural outcome. Following are some examples of the Slenderman mythos through poems, fanciful historic sources and fan fiction disguised as fact culled from various sources across the web.

The Der Ritter (The Knight) Woodcut

Der Ritter.

A German woodcut from the 1540s. It has puzzled historians since it was discovered at Halstberg castle in 1883. The woodcut bears the distinct style of a known woodcut artist from that area, Hans Freckenberg. Although know for his realistic depiction of human anatomy in his works, something that was unusual for the woodcuts in the 16th century, this picture differs radically from the rest of Freckenbergs works. The character to the right bears little semblance to a human being, with skeletal physique and long limbs at odd angles. Many theories have been discussed as to what Freckenberg wanted to symbolize with that character, some say its a personification of the religious wars that raged in Europe at the time, others say its a personification of the mysterious plague that have been believed to be the reason for the mysterious abandoning of the Halstberg castle and the nearby village in 1543.

The Dubh Fear of Old Scotland

In Scotland there is the legend of the Fear Dubh (The Black Man). This creature is said to haunt solitary footpaths at night, generally those that pass through woodland. It is reputed to be entirely malevolent. I can remember my granny telling me stories about a lot of Scottish folk tales, she only ever mentioned the Fear Dubh once, and that was in church. I was about eight, and was spending the summer holidays with her. She took me to church one Tuesday morning, and told me to wait by the font while she spoke to Father MacAndrews. And all she said was the name, and then "He's been at the bairns' window again". The priest just nodded, and said he'd be round later. I was a curious child, so I took a walk around the house later. It was built on the edge of woodland, so close that the branches of an ash tree almost touched the window. Ivy grew up the side of the house, but it was dying back in long thin patches, the leaves wrinked and sort of wet-looking. My grany made me say my prayers that night, and put her rosary beads under my pillow. And I fell asleep to the sound of wet leaves brushing against my window. And I dreamed of a thin man who looked at me, even though he had no eyes, and tried to touch me, even though he had no hands. I can't actually remember much of the next

31

few days. My mum says it was the trauma of my grans' funeral that's made those days so blurry, but I don't understand why, because I coped okay with other funerals round about that age. And I don't understand how Father MacAndrews died of a heart attack the same night (he was only thirty, and fit as a butchers' dog). And if Gran died of a stroke, I don't understand why the police sealed off the house and woodland. It wasn't the local police either; they were all big serious men in dark blue with riot gear on. You'd have thought that their presence would have meant that local vandals would have stayed away, but they didn't, and poor Grans' house got firebombed a few weeks later. The walls are still standing though. You can see the long thin streaks that the smoke's made on the white walls. Looks almost like an octopus' tentacles, reaching for you. I've still got the rosary, and even though people laugh, I sleep with it under my pillow. Because if I don't, I dream. About the sound of wet leaves sliding softly across a window, and the way he is still watching me, even though he has no eye

Schlankwald (Thin Forest)

A supposed ancient Germanic poem that according to
the source was "poorly translated" by James Rossi

They say that monsters come only at night,

That light will drive them away.

But not all creatures follow this rule,

Safety not certain during the day.

He hides on the fringes of your vision,

Brief glimpses of the distorted.

He slithers and writhes behind your eyes,

Reaching for you, limbs contorted.

Before you know it your children are taken,

 And now it's come down to you.

His breath is oppressive, his presence acidic,

He feels pity is undue.

Suddenly, trapped in his grasp so tight,

You struggle to break yourself free.

He laughs and he gurgles and he screeches with
glee,

He turns your head for you to see.

Your children are crying though their eyes are
removed,

They collapse, still and silent.

His arms and legs bend pulling you closer, The
man's eyes dark and violent.

He strikes and he cuts, your skin flays open,

Your soul to weak to resist.

This should not have happened,

if only you had listened,

Never go into his forest.

The Tale of Stela and Sorina

An old Romanian folktale by an unknown artist

Once upon a time there were twin girls, Stela and
Sorina. They were brave little girls, and had no fear
of the dark, nor of spiders and other crawling
things. Where other young ladies and even young
boys would cower, Stela and Sorina would walk
with their heads held high. They were good girls,
obedient to their mother and father and to the word
of God. They were the best children a mother could
ask for, and this was their undoing. One day, Stela
and Sorina were out with their mother gathering
berries from the forest. Their mother bid them stay

close to her, and they listened, as they were good children. The day was bright and clear, and even as they walked closer to the center of the forest the light barely dimmed. It was nearly bright as noon when they found the tall man. The tall man stood in a clearing, dressed as a nobleman, all in black. Shadows lay over him, dark as a cloudy midnight. He had many arms, all long and boneless as snakes, all sharp as swords, and they writhed like worms on nails. He did not speak, but made his intentions known. Their mother tried not to listen, but she could no more disobey the tall man than she could forget how to breathe. She walked into the clearing, her daughters shortly behind her. "Stela," she said, "take my knife, and cut a circle on the ground big enough to lie in." Stela, who was not afraid of the tall man, nor afraid of the quiver in her mother's voice, obeyed what her mother said. "Sorina," the mother said, "take the berries and spread them in the circle, and crush them underfoot until the juice stains the earth." Though Sorina wondered why her mother asked her to do such a thing, she obeyed, because she was a good girl. "Stela," the mother said, "lie in the circle." Stela, though she worried she might stain her clothes, did as her mother asked. "Sorina," the mother said, and bid Sorina cut her sister open with the knife. Sorina could not; would not. "Please," her mother said. "If you don't, it will be worse. So much worse." But Sorina could not, and she threw the knife away and ran home, crying. She hid under her bed, afraid for the first time in her life. She waited until her father came home from the fields, and told him of the terrible thing she had found in the woods. Her father comforted her, and told her she would be safe. He went to the woods, his axe in hand, and as he commanded, she stayed by the hearth, waiting for his return. After some time she fell asleep. When she woke, it was to the sound of knocking on her door at the darkest hour of the night. "Who is there?" she said.

"It is your father," the knocker said.

"I don't believe you!" said Sorina.

"It is your sister," the knocker said. "It cannot be!" said Sorina. "I am your mother," said the knocker, "and I told you it would be worse." And the door, locked tight before her father left, fell open as if it had been left ajar. And her mother stepped in, her sister's head clutched in one bloody hand, her father's in the other. "Why?" wept Sorina. "Because," said her mother, "there is no reward for goodness; there is no respite for faith; there is nothing but cold steel teeth and scourging fire for all of us. And it's coming for you now." And the tall man slid from the fire, and clenched Sorina in his burning embrace. And that was the end of her.

The Tslethenee Men of Native American Myth
An ancient American Indian story of violent and often featureless tall dark beings that sometimes kidnapped and even ate unwary children.

Small bear wandered from the campfire as the bird called from the woods.

"Why are you singing brother bird?" He asked, "It is past the time when you should sleep!"

The bird did not answer.

Small bear heard the bird once again call from deeper in the woods. It sounded very sad.

"Are you hurt or in pain, my brother?" he asked as he walked through the deep forest. "Perhaps I can help!"

Small Bear had wandered far from his camp as he sought to find the bird which cried at night. Soon the wood was dark and he could not see.

The bird's song soon turned to laughter.

Small Bear cried out in fear, "My brother, what do you want of me?"

The bird's laughter became that of a small baby as the woods grabbed Small Bear and torn him to pieces and fed on his flesh and bone. The song of the bird was no longer in the forest; instead there was only the sound of cracking bones. As the thin tongue of the Ts'el'eni licked the marrow from Small Bear's broken bones, the dark man sucked out and devoured the boy's spirit.

The Hamilton Psychiatric Hospital Document

Unknown patient from June 16, 1997 to July 17, 2004

Hamilton Psychiatric Hospital
100 West 5th St.
Hamilton, ON

Patient File – 97-213-011
Patient Name – Unknown

Supervising Doctor – Harris, J. (June 16, 1997)
Venditti, S. (August 30, 1997)

June 16, 1997 - Female subject, twenty to thirty years of age, was admitted to facility. The subject is unresponsive to verbal or physical stimulation. The woman of unknown origin was found wandering the streets earlier in the morning. She had several cuts and bruises as well as tears in her clothing. The police officers who responded suspect she may have been the victim of a mugging or sexual assault but so far the subject has been unresponsive. No identification was found on her person. The only clue to her possible origin is a receipt found in one of her pockets. The receipt, dated the morning of June 15, 1997, appears to be from a store in St. Louis, Missouri. The police say they will have to contact the store in the morning for confirmation of its origin. In the opinion of the supervising doctor the patient should be kept for observation. Copies of the police report can be found in this file as supporting document *1c: HWPS report 97017601*

June 17, 1997 – Constable Webber of the Hamilton-Wentworth Police services says the store confirmed that the transaction was indeed from their store. One of the store clerks remembered serving a patron matching the patient's description and clothing. They believe she must come here by plane, but without Identification there may be know way to trace her flight.

July 3, 1997 - Hamilton-Wentworth Police Services sent the results of their tests. There is no indication of sexual assault and wounds are not consistent with a physical attack. They believe injuries may have resulted from a scrambling escape; possibly through a wooded area due to some forest detritus found on the clothing. Copies of the police test report can be found in this file as supporting document *3a: HWPS report 97017832*

July 9, 1997 – The patient has begun to speak. Though she still remains unresponsive to questioning and physical stimulus, she has started to mumble. Most of what she says seems to be incoherent ramblings.

July 10, 1997 – The patient's rambling seem to revolve around a tall man with, as she puts it, empty eyes. Still no response to questioning.

July 15, 1997 – There was some success with the patient today. During a round of questioning she stopped her rambling and addressed the supervising doctor. Only two words were spoken directly to him before she continued rambling; "you're next". Patient is being kept under increased security due what is being perceived as a threat.

July 17, 1997 – The patient was not in her room. Security has reviewed their footage and according to them the patient was admitted to her room at 7:30 pm and did not leave through the door between that time and when the orderly came to retrieve her in the morning. There is no damage to the window or its lock. At this point it is unknown how she escaped.

August 30, 1997 – Patient's file has been transferred to Dr. Venditti due to Dr. Harris' unknown whereabouts.

July 17, 2004 – Patient file closed.

The Document reads:

Hamilton Psychiatric Hospital

100 West 5th St. Hamilton, ON

Patient File – 97-213-011 Patient Name – Unknown

Supervising Doctor – Harris, J. (June 16, 1997)

Venditti, S. (August 30, 1997)

June 16, 1997 - Female subject, twenty to thirty years of age, was admitted to facility. The subject is unresponsive to verbal or physical stimulation. The woman of unknown origin was found wandering the streets earlier in the morning. She had several cuts and bruises as well as tears in her clothing. The police officers who responded suspect she may have been the victim of a mugging or sexual assault but so far the subject has been unresponsive. No identification was found on her person. The only clue to her possible origin is a receipt found in one of her pockets. The receipt, dated the morning of June 15, 1997, appears to be from a store in St. Louis, Missouri. The police say they will have to contact the store in the morning for confirmation of its origin. In the opinion of the supervising doctor the patient should be kept for observation. Copies of the police report can be found in this file as supporting document *1c: HWPS report 97017601*

June 17, 1997 – Constable Webber of the Hamilton-Wentworth Police services says the store confirmed that the transaction was indeed from their store. One of the store clerks remembered serving a patron matching the patient's description and clothing. They believe she must come here by plane, but without Identification there may be know way to trace her flight.

July 3, 1997 – Hamilton-Wentworth Police Services sent the results of their tests. There is no indication of sexual assault and wounds are not consistent with a physical attack. They believe injuries may have resulted from a scrambling escape; possibly through a wooded area due to some forest detritus found on the clothing. Copies of the police test report can be found in this file as supporting document *3a: HWPS report 97017832*

July 9, 1997 – The patient has begun to speak. Though she still remains unresponsive to questioning and physical stimulus, she has started to mumble. Most of what she says seems to be incoherent ramblings.

July 10, 1997 – The patient's rambling seem to revolve around a tall man with, as she puts it, empty eyes. Still no response to questioning.

July 15, 1997 – There was some success with the patient today. During a round of questioning she stopped her rambling and addressed the supervising doctor. Only two words were spoken directly to him before she continued rambling; "you're next". Patient is being kept under increased security due what is being perceived as a threat.

July 17, 1997 – The patient was not in her room. Security has reviewed their footage and according to them the patient was admitted to her room at 7:30 pm and did not leave through the door between that time and when the orderly came to retrieve her in the morning. There is no damage to the window or its lock. At this point it is unknown how she escaped.

August 30, 1997 – Patient's file has been transferred to Dr. Venditti due to Dr. Harris' unknown whereabouts.

July 17, 2004 – Patient file closed.

The Unknown Stalker

I spend a lot of my time outside at night cause I work till 3 AM and sleep in the morning. I walk back home just because I like being alone at night, and I usually carry my s**t 15 year old camera with me I usually walk down the middle of the road cause it's a weird feeling, you know, no f***ing cars or whatever. I was snapping pictures tonight when all of a sudden this tall guy walks out from the eastern road of the intersection. I mean, a f***ing business suit, 3 f***ing AM. So I figure maybe he's drunk, really well-balanced drunk, because he walks really f***ing slow and looks straight ahead. I mean this guy moves so slow it's creepy and unnatural. There's something off about his silhouette too. He stops somewhere in the middle of the intersection and i take a picture, cause

damn this is f***ing weird. I only noticed after I
went through them that he's f***ing looking at me!
you can see his head is turned...

Well, I'm not in the mood to get raped tonight or
anything, so I turn around and speedwalk up the
hill. At the top there's an old gas station that's been
closed for 5 years and a parking lot, and I have to
cross the lot on my way home. I still feel my skin

crawling after seeing that dude so just to make sure
I turn around and there he f***ing is.

I mean f***ing seriously, this guy must be wearing
running shoes cause I didn't hear a single f***ing
step and my ears are pretty good. Not to mention
there's no other sound whatsoever. I'm sure men's
dress shoes make noise even if you're trying to be
quiet. I'm freaking out now, because this is really

f***ing odd. Not to mention he looks like he's holding rope or some f***ing thing, I mean look at the silhouette. So I start running. I was hoping I'd lose him cause it really is foggy, and it's a neighborhood where you can easily get lost if you aren't familiar with it. Whatever amount of time later, I look back (this was seriously at least a mile away from the parking lot):

What the f***. I realize that besides for when he walked to the middle of the intersection, I have not

46

seen this guy f***ing move. When I turn around
he's just standing there. I just ran over a mile, and
presumably so did he, and I can't even see him
breathing. F** all. And you can see whatever the
f*** he's holding better here. What is that, f***ing
rope? At this point I figure f*** it, I'm going to run
flat out, all the way home because I'm close now
and I prefer this f*** not to know where I live. I
start running and I get the idea to take some pictures
just for the hell of it, I mean what if this dude starts
following me around tomorrow? I only got one that
wasn't blurred all to f***.

Goons, what the f*** is that. Those f***ing trees
behind him are old and pretty goddamn tall. The

dude could have torn the top leaves off of them. His magical f***ing no-sound shoes are at least 6 feet off the ground. I can't f***ing see what it is that's keeping him up but it looks like whatever I thought was rope before. I can bet he wasn't moving when I took the picture because the motion blur is pretty much the same for the background as it is for him. What the f***. It's early morning right now and I think the sun's coming up, but I can't f***ing tell for sure because every window is locked, every shade is drawn. I keep hearing tapping sounds on the window. I thought it was the tree in my backyard at first (its branches sometimes touch both the first and second floor back windows) but the tapping came from the front. And there isn't any f***ing wind. I'm making GBS threads myself here. Dammit, what do I do?

Unknown Government Document

Shows the military is aware of the Slenderman issue and are covering it up.

Massive tree, previously not witnessed to be crushed, was now lying across the beach, several branches floated in the surfline. S. Man momentarily reappeares, gives an ear-piercing scream and vanishes. Sign-off at 19:50 ▓▓▓▓▓▓▓▓▓

The loss of facility 0003 at ▓▓▓ was not a wholly unexpected, and more similar characteristics to the partial compromise of 0005 earlier last year. Unlike 0005, 0003 is a complete loss and ▓▓▓ along with her full test team and personal are missing.

Project head ▓▓▓▓▓▓ at 0001 in ▓▓▓▓▓▓ has decided to suspend all normal operations at 0002 and 0004-0028 following elimination of all human ▓▓▓▓▓ at each facility. Subject 1 to remain in standby until further notice.

0001 in tandem with Main Hall and Circulatory Roots will begin dissemination of KEY and KAGI to prearranged social intersections along with the LOSUNG. With the so-called "Web 2.0 ▓▓▓▓▓▓▓▓▓▓▓

quantum biologists feel that this will raise our herd mental resistance of ▓▓▓ by raising the collective consciousness of Social Alpha and ▓▓▓▓▓▓▓▓▓▓▓

Propagation to increase incident rate by ▓▓▓ percent. Expected casualties to in the range of ▓▓▓ but ▓▓ is our acceptable upper limit.

20-year-old Skier Found Dead After Month-Long Search.

JASPER, Alta. -

The body of a 20-year-old woman has been found after a month-long search in the Rockies west of Jasper.

RCMP and park officials confirm the body to be that of missing skier Amanda Fischer, who has not been seen since leaving on a trip with three friends in early January.

Her remains were discovered today by park officials. Reports suggest her body was found contorted, and in an advanced state of decay, high in a tree. Investigators have refused to comment how her body could have been left in such a condition.

On January 10th, Fischer, along with boyfriend Douglas Bellanger, 21, and friend Natasha Pierce, 20, left their cabin at Mica Mountains Resort. That was the last time they were seen alive.

A second friend, 22-year-old Thomas Chambers left them a day before the disappearance, to return to Calgary, allegedly due to health concerns. He was questioned by RCMP two days after the other three were declared missing.

During questioning Chambers allegedly told officers that he had left the other three and returned home due to recurring night-terrors featuring a tall man in black peering in through his cabin's window.

Investigators confirmed they had ruled Chambers out as a possible suspect, but considered him a key witness. A source within the RCMP, who spoke on condition of anonymity, revealed to the Calgary Sun that officers had confiscated a digital camera and a camcorder at the time of the interview, which were never returned.

RCMP have been unable to question Chambers further, as he himself has been missing since January 21st. His home was found ransacked that morning, and he has not been seen since.

The hunt continues for information or clues that could lead investigators to the location, or bodies, of Bellanger, Pierce and Chambers. The disappearances are considered linked, but RCMP refuse to comment further. (Cal Sun)(The Canadian Press)"

Missing Girl Case

Stirling City Post posted:
Rash of Animal Mutilations Blamed on Coyotes.
By Tom Chisolm
Posted: April 21, 1987
Stirling City, CA - A rash of pet deaths in northern Stirling City over the past several weeks has been blamed on coyotes, according to the Butte County Animal Control Department.
"After a particularly harsh winter, food supplies may be low, forcing wild animals to venture into town in search of prey," Animal Control Officer Joel Driscol said.

As many as nine dogs and cats have gone missing since January, and have been found in various states of decay. Many of the pets were disemboweled, or otherwise seriously mutilated.

"It was unusual, I'll admit," Driscol said in an interview. "The wounds were unusually precise, and it's rare that a wild animal would leave so much of the carcass uneaten."

"My daughters are extremely upset by this,' said David Elkins, owner of the most recent victim, "They're ten and eight, and don't fully understand what's happened to [the cat]."

Stirling City Post posted:
Police Have Few Leads in Missing Girl Case
By Will Higgins
Posted: June 15, 1987
Stirling City, CA - A spokesman for the Stirling City Police Department admitted this week that there were no promising leads in the case of eight year old Katrina Elkins, who went missing from her home Thursday night. "It's like she disappeared into thin air," said neighbor and family friend, Marybeth Carlisle.

Police were called to the residence at 6:30 AM on Friday morning by Katrina's father, David. He realized that Katrina was missing when he went into her bedroom to wake her for school and discovered that she was not in her bed.

The only possible witness was the victim's sister, ten year old Alice, with whom Katrina shares a bedroom. Alice has been unable to provide many details to investigators, however.

"It seems that [the girl] suffers from an overactive imagination," SCPD Sergeant William Hohne said, "she told us the last time she saw her sister, was through the window where she was 'hugging the tall man'."

According to witness statements, over the past several weeks a man had been coming to the girls' bedroom window at night, where he would tap on the glass, 'make faces', and watch the girls.

Police investigators initially dismissed the account as a dream, as the bedroom window is on the second story, with no support beneath it.

"[Alice] Elkins reported that, on the night of her sisters disappearance, they were again awakened by a tapping at the glass," Sergeant Hohne explained, "She heard her sister get out of bed, and have a short conversation. When she didn't hear her sister get back in bed after several minutes, she got up and went to the window, where she saw her sister in the side yard, 'hugging the tall man'. According to the witness, the man looked up at her, grinned, and indicated that she was to come down as well with a 'snaky arm'. It was at this point that Miss Elkins became extremely frightened, and returned to bed. The tapping continued for some minutes, but finally ceased." Police scoured the Elkins' yard for clues, with no success. When asked why Alice had not told her parents about the tall men before, she explained, "He scared me. He told us to not tell Mom and Dad, or we'd be in trouble. He told us that he was our friend, and that he would give us anything we wanted, but we had to keep his secret. His smile was scary... and his voice. He said nice things but he sounded mean." Police believe that there is no link between the disappearance and the vicious killing of the Elkin's cat by disemboweling in April.

The Hans Freckengburg woodcut and
Slenderman's Eternal Curse

Another woodcut dated to around the 1540's. Its the
work of Hans Freckenberg who disappeared in 1543
in Halstedt. The entity to the right is very similar to

the odd humanoid from Freckenbergs earlier woodcut; 'DER RITTER' since both share many of the same features such as unnatural height and long limbs. One thing to point out is that much work went into the entity to the right, at the cost of the depiction of the people to the left and middle in the woodcut wich is very crude, something that is quite unusual for Freckenberg who was best know for his lifelike depictions of humans in his earlier works. The reason for this sudden change of priorities in Freckenberg's style are still a topic of hot debate. Okay… I've been pondering this all day. Let me preface this by saying that I am an extremely skeptical person. I do not believe in God, I do not believe in fairies, I don't believe in magic and I think stories about "alien abductions" or conspiracy theories are irritating beyond belief because so many people waste their time believing them. My job requires me to think of cases in terms of proof – I am a biologist, and unfortunately I get confronted with all sorts of kooky theories more than I'd like. But I've never been able to get a grip on the following story, which has haunted me for years. I'm still not sure what it is, and I never had a name for it until I came across oblique references to the "Slender Man" from a friend who's interested in cryptozoology (and who forwards me this kind of stuff just to annoy me). As a kid, I used to live in a rural area that only really got urbanized in the early '90s. Apart from the village's main road and a few smaller roads, the east of the village was a dense, murky forest and the west of the village was bordered by the Scheldt River. Since the Scheldt had been more or less straightened out by engineers a long time before I was born, a lot of its former anabranches had been cut off and had become marshes. Further uphill from the marshes were a number of farms, extensive wheat fields, grassy plains and an abandoned brickyard. We used to live in one of the oldest houses in the village, so creaky floors, cracks in the walls that produced strangely melodious sounds when it was storming, or generally strange movements and sounds outside the house at night were pretty common, and I was used to them even as a toddler. I slept in a particularly noisy bedroom with a very high ceiling, a very tall door and a large window. One of my only memories of this room is quite a terrifying one.

When I was about five years old, I awoke in the middle of the night because my window had been blown open by a strong gust of wind. Now, I probably would've gone back to sleep because I was used to the sound and the feeling of the chilly autumn wind, but this time I heard and felt nothing. A very strong sensation of terror gripped me, and I wanted to scream for my parents, but found that I couldn't speak a word, nor make any sort of movement. At that moment, the door to my bedroom opened with a very loud bang, and in the opening, lit in the back by the dimmed lights from the hallway, stood a vaguely human figure so tall that it easily filled up the available space. The figure looked impossibly slim, and its legs seemed to fade away near the ground, while its arms were flung wide and far. Although I couldn't discern any sort of feature, I got the dizzying sensation that it was looking at me. Then, I heard its voice, which didn't seem to emanate from its mouth, nor did it feel like it was directly speaking in my mind – rather, its voice came from all over the room simultaneously, surrounding me. Its sound was very deep and disjointed, as if someone was speaking through a metal tube. The creature thundered the word "Jozef" at me. Jozef used to be a fairly common Dutch name. When the creature then started shrieking at me, I somehow regained control of my voice, closed my eyes and screeched at the top of my lungs. I only opened my eyes again when I heard my parents dashing up the stairs. The creature was gone. As I came of age, I dismissed this experience as an extremely vivid nightmare, possibly even a hallucination, since I became very ill the next day, and according to my mother, I had an abnormally high fever. The only thing that haunted me about the story, which I couldn't erase from my mind, was that when my parents were running up the stairs, my door was still wide open, while I knew that it had been shut when I fell asleep. I nearly forgot about this ordeal until I was about 20 and started inquiring about my family history. I was asking my mother a few questions, purely out of curiosity. This mainly had to do with the peculiar fact that a lot of her male ancestors died at a very young age – she was a baby when her father had died due to stomach cancer, she was a toddler when her uncle died in a car crash, and she'd never known her mother's father because he'd died in 1947. My great-grandfather's brother died young as well, in a freak accident while watching a lightning storm from the window of his bedroom – he was struck by lightning and killed on the spot. Another one of her great-uncles drowned in the Scheldt after losing a wager to see who could swim fastest after lunch. Nearly all of them were local villagers and farmers. Now, as I was asking about my great-grandfather, whose fate piqued my interest, my mother became very dismissive, and told me I wouldn't want to know the story behind his untimely death, since "it was an ugly mess". Obviously, her attempts to not speak about it only increased my interest, if only because I had in fact known my great-grandmother for a short period, and she, too had refused to talk about her deceased husband. So eventually, my mother told me the story. In 1940, Belgium was occupied by Nazi Germany. Because my future great-grandmother, whose name was Agnes, and her husband had a big grocery store on a transit road between two villages, their house was chosen by the Germans as a makeshift garrison. My family hated it. They spoke only very little German, and the soldiers made no effort to learn any Dutch. They treated my family as if they were mentally incapacitated yokels, and ate all of their food. There was one exception, however – a young soldier named Peter, who was actually interested in the village and frequently asked for directions to the best walking routes through the nearby forests and marshes. Grudgingly, my great-grandfather accompanied him, but over the next months, they hesitantly developed some sort of friendship, because it turned out that Peter not only was an adamant trekker who loved being outdoors, he was also an amateur photographer, just like my great-grandfather. In the late Summer of 1942, something terrible happened. One evening, my great-grandfather and Peter were exploring the marshes and taking a few pictures. A few hours later, well past midnight, my great-grandfather came home, looking like an utter maniac, wide-eyed and sweaty, shaking and unable to utter a coherent word. The other Germans in the house were very alarmed, and while two of them guarded my great-grandfather, the rest went to look for Peter. From what my mother told me (and she heard the story from her own mother, who was about 9 years old at that time), the Germans came back in the early morning with some of Peter's equipment, visibly shaking and completely silent. The next day, they took my great-grandfather, who was still dazed and alternated between screaming fits and apathy, with them and relocated to another house. My great-grandfather was sent to a German factory where lots of young Belgians were forcibly sent, because he was blamed for Peter's death*, even though the local commander admitted to Agnes that they knew he hadn't killed him. The commander hoped that my great-grandfather would "straighten out" again under the heavy routine of the labor there. He was wrong. In 1946, one year after the war had ended, my great-grandfather came back home. He had obviously been treated very badly at the factory. He was completely emaciated, had a bunch of nasty scars and was deathly exhausted. The worst thing was, he was now completely apathetic to anything. He mostly didn't eat and slept a lot, stared off into space or went on strange long walks without explaining where he had gone. The day before he died, he destroyed nearly all of his old stuff, and

ripped out all pictures of all albums he had collected
– he only kept one picture, which he paraded around
the house like a lunatic, constantly pointing at it:
"It's him! It's him!" he kept repeating, until he
collapsed on the living room floor and drifted off
into a coma. The next day, he died. My great-
grandmother wanted to burn that last picture, but
my future grandmother managed to salvage it, and
later kept it in her attic. Last year, after she had
died, I quietly searched her house for the picture…
and I found it. I wish I never had. The horror of my
encounter with the terrifying creature, the "Slender
Man" as you all call him, came back in full force.
You can call me stupid for only making the
connection at that moment, but my great-
grandfather's name was Jozef. I apologize for the
bad quality of the picture, but it was pretty wasted
when I found it, and my scanner is a piece of junk. I
have a higher-resolution image available on request.
* In my village's official history, Peter's death was
described as an accident. The official explanation
was that he had sunk into a pile of gravel while on
watchout, and suffocated. This is ostensibly untrue,
because there was no need for watchouts in my

village in 1942, and no soldier in their right mind would think of a pile of gravel as a good lookout spot.

Historical Archetypes for Slenderman

While there have been multiple attempts by the multimedia fan fiction community to connect Slenderman to various historical legends, many of these attempts are misleading, outright dramatic revisionism or hoaxes.

Such is the case for the "Der Ritter" woodcut.

In the mythos it is attributed to a famous woodcutter named Hans Freckenberg. But not only was there no famous woodcutter by the name of Hans Freckenberg, this illustration is actually a photo manipulation of a famous woodcutting by an actual famous artist by the name of Georg Scharffenberg.

The original Der Ritter woodcut shows a traditional visage of death piercing a knight in his abdomen with a lance.

The original Der Ritter woodcut was originally part of a medieval pamphlet called "***Der Todten-Tantz***" (The Dance of Death). According to "The Spirit of the Ages" website, this pamphlet included 41 illustrations produced on woodcuts to designs by Hans Holbein

that are thought to have been prepared prior to 1526. Hans Lützelburger , a distinguished woodcut specialist of the time, has been identified as the artisan responsible for preparing Holbein's designs for printing. The 1st Edition of these prints was produced in 1538 by the brothers Trechsel.

The French description provided on the title page, "Les Simulachres & Historiées Faces de la Mort avtant elegamtment pourtraictes, que artificiellement imaginées" may be translated to English as "The Images and Storied Aspects of Death, as elegantly delineated as they are ingeniously imaged".

Throughout Holbein's suite, Death is shown escorting people from all walks of life to their final destiny. The implied message provided by the suite is that all must live their lives virtuously and be prepared, as Death may visit without warning. This theme is one that developed strongly through the 15th and 16th Centuries and is likely to have grown from the highly visible nature of death, especially in the years following the devastating plague known as the "Black Death".[2]

The "Der Ritter" image carries the monogram "GS" and so is commonly attributed to contributing artist Georg Scharffenberg. This illustration is traditionally associated with the poetic text,

Death to the Knight:
Mr Knight, you have been written down,
That you must practice chivalry.
With Death and his servants,
It helps you neither to struggle nor fight.
The Knight:

---

[2] http://spiritoftheages.com/Hans%20Holbein%20-%20"Der%20Todten-Tantz".htm last accessed 519/2012

I, as a stern knight,

Have served the world well with noble mind.

Now I have been, against Knight's Orders,

Coerced to this dance.[3]

Another close association to the Der Ritter woodcut is the "Der Großmann" legend of Germany. Der Großmann literally means "The Great Man" and there is no such legend in German history.

While the Der Ritter woodcut is a proven hoax, it does show a close connection to the true archetype of Slenderman, death itself.

Death is an unrelenting force. It is unstoppable, it is inevitable. There is no escape. It is no respecter of persons, taking the very rich and the poor alike. From the day we are born, we are destined for the grave. Our life is a measured clock, and as each second is counted down the dark visage of death draws closer and closer. There is nothing we can do about it. Oh, we can try to extend our life by natural

---

3

http://spiritoftheages.com/The%20Knight%20(Der%20Todten -Tantz;%20or,%20The%20Dance%20of%20Death)%20- %20illustrated%20by%20Georg%20Scharffenberg.htm Last accessed 5/19/2012 and unnatural means. But sometimes the sickle of the Grim Reaper strikes when you least expect it. We are all destined to rot in the grave and become but dust.

Death scares all of us. Even the most faithful with religious certainty still holds doubts about what lies beyond the grave. Death is the end, even if you believe in an after life.

The Biblical text tells us that man was originally created perfect and without sin. He was to be immortal. After the creation of man God told Adam, *"And the Lord God commanded the man, saying, "Of every tree of the garden you may freely eat; but of the tree of the knowledge of good and evil you shall not eat, for in the day that you eat of it you shall surely die."*[4]
And of course, man disobeyed and ate of that tree. Satan disguised as a serpent tempted Eve and Eve talked Adam into disobedience. So in essence, the tree was the instrument of death for all mankind. According to the Biblical literature, there was no

---

[4] Genesis 2:16-17

death before the fruit of the tree was eaten. Death came to man in the form of a tree.

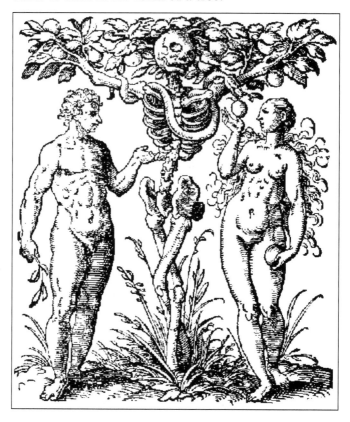

Slenderman incorporates the thematic elements of the Biblical death tree that has been passed down for to us for hundreds of generations. It is imbedded into our subconscious and has been brought forth in thousands of metaphors throughout the ages. To many of us just the phrase "Dark Forest" gives us the chills.

Just as the Grim Reaper strikes down every mortal with its reaper's sickle, Slenderman reaches out with his extended arms and twisted tree like limbs to ensnare us.

Like death, Slenderman stalks us from childhood and he will inevitably get us. He is unstoppable. He is beyond our control, a supernatural juggernaut with a singular focus. Like death, you know it is coming; it is always lurking in the dark corner ready to pounce on you at any time. There is no escape. It will only stop when it consumes your life.

Slenderman is death incarnate.

The Slenderman myth strikes us at the core of our being. We are, after all is said and done, helpless. Once we know it is stalking us, it will remain on our periphery for the rest of our lives. We are destined for that fateful encounter one day, and how it will strike us remains a gruesome mystery.

Another less universal stereotypical archetype of Slenderman is a more modern one that may have old roots.

The Men in Black phenomena is a decidedly modern variant of medieval tales of encounters with the "black man".

In Washington Irving's story "The Devil and Tom Walker[5]" set in 1727, Irving tells how Tom asks "the black man" who he really is. The man tells Tom that he goes by many names and is called the black miner or sometimes the black woodsman. Since the Indians are gone, he presides over the persecutions of various religious sects, supports slave-dealers and is the master of the Salem witches. Tom replies that he must be "Old Scratch", which is another name for the devil, and the black man acknowledges that he is indeed the devil himself, Old Scratch.

---

[5] Irving, Washington (1824). "The Devil and Tom Walker". *Tales of a Traveller*. ISBN 9780805785159.

This Washington Irving tale reflects an old tradition of the devil coming in the guise of a man dressed in black to deceive and ensnare the unwary. The black attire itself has a double meaning, since not only is the color black associated with evil but it is also the primary color of clergy and priests at the time after the Reformation.

The Men in Black associated with the UFO phenomenon has much in common with the classic old tales of the black man.

The Men in Black phenomenon actually started before Kenneth Arnold's famous sighting of flying saucers near Mount Rainier, Washington on June 24, 1947. On June 21, 1947 near Maury Island, Washington, Harbor master Harold Dahl spotted six UFOs from his patrol boat. The UFOs had buzzed his boat and covered it in metal fragments. Dahl reported the incident to his supervisor, Fred Lee Crisman, who preserved some of the metal residue. After the Arnold incident made UFOs a national story just days later, Dahl had the first recorded encounter with the modern Men in Black. Dahl told reporters that soon after his sighting he had been warned not to tell his story to anyone, or there would be dire consequences. This individual was completely dressed in black. Dahl had obviously seen something that these Men in Black did not want him to see. But who were they?

Dahl experience might have been a mere footnote in UFO history if it was not for the 1956 publication of *"They Knew Too Much About Flying Saucers"* by author Gray Barker. In this ground breaking book, Gray relates the story of Al. K. Bender of Connecticut who had a similar encounter with the odd Men in Black. Gray's narrative of this encounter set the pace for what is now the stereotypical M.I.B. story: Someone sees a UFO and tries to go public. Suddenly, odd men in black suits pull up in a big black car to threaten the witness. Thus the witness is too frightened to tell anyone about his encounter lest they meet a sudden demise. Were these government officials from the CIA, FBI or some unknown intelligence organization? Or were they something else entirely?

The Men in Black as described by these witnesses in the 50s and 60s are an odd sort of creature. Many witnesses claimed that they felt these beings were not quit human. They had a bizarre skin color that was not quite ethnic, but rather it was just plain unnatural. They sometimes moved as if their limbs were not attached the same way as normal humans limbs were. To others their movement seemed as if it was robotic. They wore sunglasses at night and indoors; if they took them off, witnesses described that they possessed inhuman eyes. Their mannerism were also perplexing, it seemed as if they were out of place and unaccustomed to many facets of modern day life. Some seemed fascinated with the ordinary functions of ball point pens or even pencils. Many also were perplexed at the human consumption of food.

The cars that the Men in Black drove also had odd properties. Their long black cars made no noise, had no tailpipes and seemed to glide over the ground instead of moving on their wheels.

Like Slenderman, the Men in Black appeared to be something…other. While they dwelt in our reality, it would seem that they were from… elsewhere.

Like Men in Black, Slenderman is threatening.

Like Men in Black, and encounter with Slenderman is dreadful and life changing.

Encountering either of these other worldly beings has to dire consequences.

Real Slenderman Encounters

As I related in the introduction, after I first read about Slenderman, I had an odd feeling. Not only was it the unearthly feeling of being observed by an Eldritch being of supernatural power; it was a feeling that I had encountered this entity before.

Most of my life I have heard many an odd story of the unknown. From missionaries to Fortean investigators, for the last 35+ years I have heard a plethora of stories involving entities, demonic presences and aliens. Within the last 5 years since I have begun to write about the unexplained on my blog "The Paranormal Pastor" there has been a steady flow of these encounters crossing my desk.

After reading of Slenderman, I realized that even before the being was "created" on the Internet, people from all walks of life had been encountering this creature in one way or the other. And since the Mem became famous, these encounters have multiplied exponentially. Here are a few of these stories categorized in three sections. These are

General Encounters, Specific Encounters and Alien Encounters. The General Encounters are encounters with an entity that fits within the description and actions of the Slenderman of the mythos. Specific Encounters are stories that fit perfectly into the mythos as an actual encounter with Slenderman. And lastly, Alien Encounters are the Slenderman type encounter that deals with connections to UFOs or alien abductions.

General Encounters.

"Dear Pastor:

I stumbled onto your website much by accident and was intrigued by the 'Slenderman' story. I have vivid memories from childhood regarding a throng of these people emerging from the woods near our house, which was about a quarter mile from the edge of a large state forest in *(place withheld at the request of the individual)*. As a child growing up in the 1950s, my mom always warned me about "gypsies" who occasionally made their way through our neighborhood. Even so, I was intrigued nevertheless. I recall one occasion quite vividly. I was about 4 or 5 years old, playing in the back yard. I recall going into the garage, which was separate from our house. I became aware of a swishing sound, like someone walking through tall grass. I glanced out the garage window and saw an entire line of these 'Slender people' coming out of the woods just beyond our neighbor's house. They were heading our way. I was momentarily frozen. What do I do now? Fearful the "gypsies" might carry me away, I retreated into a corner of the garage and watched the procession through a crack in the wall. This was something out of storybook land! They were all slender, but some were taller than others. A few wore scarves, but their garb appeared drab with colors faded. There were a few slenders of small stature, whom I took to be children. They were holding the hands of the ones wearing scarves. I could not see their faces, but I recall their fingers were exceeding long. When they crossed into our backyard, they continued walking single file in zombie-like fashion. When they reached the coal shed (which was behind the house but about 10 feet from the garage) they divided into two lines. One line went between the coal shed and the house. The other passed between the coal shed and the garage. They continued in their slow, relentless pace, walking past the side of our house, down the road and up the hill in their slow, plodding fashion. As soon as they were out of sight, I rushed into the house. My mother immediately locked all the doors and drew all the window shades until my dad came home from work. Over the intervening years, I have often wondered about that day. Who were those strange people? Where did they come from? Where were they going? Your photo triggered recollections of that afternoon in the garage, but I saw more than just a shadow person. I saw the whole clan!"

From June of 2010:

"Dear Pastor Swope,

…every night since the start of June, between 12 and 4 in the morning I get a phone call from my ex-girlfriend. She has been attacked or being stalked by a ghost or something more. Let me tell you a bit about her before I go any further. She has severe depression, insomnia. She also has some mental trauma, what kind I will not say, because that is between me and her but as far as I know, that could

be the entire reason why this is happening.
Anyways since I've been dating her, a person she
calls "The Man" has been giving her distress.
Apparently he's been around a lot longer then I've
known her, but she says that it wasn't that bad when
she was younger. Her first experience with "The
Man" around 7 or 8, she would see a man with no
real face, just a body and a blank mass where a face
was, in her backyard standing by the fence. Not
really believing in ghosts, she freaked out and
called her mom saying there was a person outside,
when her mom got there, she seen a glimpse of a
person before he vanished behind the fence. How
much of this is true, I dont really know, I was just
told these stories by her family when I came over
now and again. . About a year ago, she called up
around midnight complaining of "The Man". She
said she could feel some one watching her through
her windows, and she wouldn't get out from under
her covers to turn on a light or do anything. But
back then I was her boyfriend and had to fight the
big bad monsters for her, so I had to couch her on
what to do and when to do it so she wouldn't be
scared. I would always tell her its ok and that she

will be fine. There were several instances where I believe either she was possessed or just the trauma of her past affected her to the point where she developed a split personality. Its also a reason why I think the trauma and 'The Man' are linked. I could immediately tell something was different because of her eyes. Normally they were a pretty blue, but then they were cold and grey. Finally after we broke up after three years in January, the man seemed to disappear. Up until June she talked to me occasionally but never past midnight. But now she calls every night between 12 and 4 complaining of The Man. I guess he's been watching her more and more. Every night he looks through her window or watches from the woods when she walks through her house…"

From an anonymous comment on my blog dated January 12, 2010 that in part reads:

" My name is____. I am being hunted by a shadow creature. It is tall and thin and tries to catch me in its long arms. I saw it in a dream, and now it is real.

All I see in the face are two eyes, and when I look in them those arms try to get me."

From a blog Comment on
July 20, 2011 10:31 AM

"My little brother use to see things like this when he was a kid of about 5 years old. He called them the 'red man' or the 'blue man' referring to their overall monochrome skinsuit type of appearance. They would show up peeking around corners or sneaking off in the peripheral of his vision. Now 26, he still has clear memories of these entities when I ask him about it."

Another blog comment:
July 22, 2011 11:43 AM
Susan G. said...
"While not a traditional Slenderman story, I have a similar one that comes from my late sister-in-law that happened to her in the sixties. She vividly remembered one time late at night when she was a kid, someone was lurking outside her door which had a tiny window at the top of it. She said she

could see the shadow of his feet from under the door, and in the top window a black top hat. From the height of the window on the door, it appears he must've been an incredibly tall man. When I read the article, it instantly called up the memory of her telling me about it back in the eighties. It spooked the heck out of me."

From notes taken at a missionary meeting at New City Alliance Church in the fall of 1987. Parentheses mark the filling of probable details from the partial notes:
"The boys had come running out of the jungle next to the missionary compound, (they were) screaming and crying about a dark shadow man that had followed them from the deep (part of the jungle). They were screaming it was like (a) 'feedip fangjenza (another word too scribbled to read)" which is a Frankenstein (monster), but it was (made) out of shadows. It was very tall and (had) long arms that (tried to?) grab them from far (away). They were sure it was right behind them. (My) wife and I went with the boys (to the) forest edge and prayed against this demon and nothing

came out of the woods (of) course. They (the boys) had nightmares for weeks (afterward), but we assured them there was nothing (to be) alarmed about, Jesus would protect them."

From a letter dated August 2009:
JoAnne wrote,
"…from childhood I have seen this demonic figure. He is a tall shadow. He has no face, but he has long arms. Out of the corner of my eye on certain nights I see him and his arms seem to be reaching out to me, and when I turn to look at him, the thing is gone. I have the real feeling that if I don't turn around to look at him his arms will catch me up and I will die.

My Father used to hit me. I was abused for the smallest things. He drank a lot and had a temper. I was frightened of my Dad, but one time I was scared out of my wits when as he was smacking me on my butt I saw myself being beat in the mirror. Behind my Dad was that tall shadow man on the back of the wall. I know it wasn't my Father's shadow, he was spanking me, but the shadow mans arms were hanging at his side. I have felt like maybe this demon inspired my father to beat me. Maybe it was a demon of anger?

I don't know. But a lot of times my Dad would take me to the bar to get drunk, and drive home. He was almost in a wreck a lot fo times and I told him I wanted to stay home after he slid the car into a ditch one time. Anyway, one time when he was drinking and I was alone I saw the shadow man outside my window. Our front yard has no trees or tall things that would cast a shadow like that. I knew it was him. I ran to my room which was upstairs, but when I looked in the window, it was up there too. Same thing when I ran to the bathroom. So I hid in my closet for hours until my Dad came home. Sometimes it seems like he is trying to reach out and grab me, but I notice the shadow before it gets to me. I am afraid that he is stalking me, and that one day I will not be able to catch him trying to snatch me up. This fills me with such fear, word can't describe. Sometimes I think I am going nuts. I feel like he is going to get me when I don't expect it. Some nights I can't sleep, noises outside make me jump. When the wind cranks up and things start to rattle, I am so scared. I need help!"

From an email that I received after the last story was published on my blog:

"I'd rather leave myself nameless, but here it goes I'm a 13 year old girl and I've been seeing this thing ever since I was about 8. Just last night I remember I was having a nightmare. The only thing I remember from the dream was waking up after his arms started coming after me. When I read about the other girl who got abused when she was young I can relate. I still am somewhat abused, but it doesn't happen as often. Other then that I was taking a picture outside today and he appeared. He was just so casually placed in the back round. I soon felt really sick after seeing him in the back round, so I went inside. After that around 4 my Mom told me to look outside to see if my brothers girlfriend's car was pulling in and he was standing there and then he snapped his head in my direction. After that I closed the blinds and just told my Mom they pulled up with everyone in the can my brother, his girlfriend and his friends. Around 5 he and 2 of his friends went for a walk and said they saw some what of a tall man next to my window after they re-looked at it, it was gone. I'm not sure if I should take this as attempt's to come after me or simple paranoia."

July 20, 2011 11:29 PM
Karpindur said...
"This dude used to give me fits when I was 15-16 years old.
One day I decided that I had enough, and decided to ignore him. I made up my mind that no matter what he did, he was not going to frighten me and I would just pretend like he didn't exist.
This seemed to really piss him off, and he began showing up everywhere, all of the time. I could feel his anger, and I enjoyed it. I knew i was getting to him for once, and it felt great. I almost, but not quite, lost all fear of him.
We moved from Cocoa Beach to LA when i was in tenth grade. We drove there taking I-10 from Florida to California, and the dude was there the whole trip. He would show alongside the road, and

running alongside the car, or standing out in the desert etc for the entire trip.

I enrolled in 10th grade at North High in Torrance that year, and was very shy and withdrawn back then. I used to hide in the library at lunch because i had no friends and felt very awkward.

One day i was standing at the card catalog as the Dude stood sort of behind me, but off to my right side. Something felt different this day about him. He was really, really mad and I got the impression he was going to try something. I ignored him, but could feel his rage, and began to wonder if I had played this game with him too long. I pulled the catalog drawer almost all of the way out and pretended to look through the cards as I watched him out of the corner of my eye. suddenly, he seemed to swell and grow taller, even though he was already well over six feet tall, and he began to run at me. He opened his arms wide like he was going to wrap me up and he seemed to be wearing a cape of some sort. He came at me with enraged intent and I forgot all about where I was. I turned to face him just as he was about to reach me. The catalog drawer fell on the floor and index cards went everywhere. I screamed and put my arms out to block him just as he reached me and wrapped that opened that cape thing so widely that it blocked out the light....

And then he was gone.

Other kids were starring at me and I was breathing hard as my heart was beat a mile a minute. There were index cards all over the floor. I didnt know what to do, so I went to the table where I left my books, gathered them up, and left. As I cleared the door I could hear an woman yell "Hey!" but I kept going as fast as i could.

I have not seen the dude since, but my 16 year old daughter has, and in our house no less.

I have not mentioned the what I went through to her, only to advise her to "just ignore him".

Who is this thing?"

From a blog comment:

September 28, 2011 10:15 PM

 Anonymous said...

"Saw something at least quite looking like it when i was a child.

One thing looking like it appeared twice near some bookshelfs with glasses on a dark part of my house. It also appeared on another room at night and another time when i looked at a mirror on my bedroom at 00:00 after hearing strange noises when i woke up. That time i didnt turn the lights on when i was gonna check and i saw that thing just behind me. Later when i was 13 it happened to me to see it on a corridor of my house.

I really dont know if all these times my mind was playing with me, because my house is really very cold, big and dark .sometimes i think it can really be paranormal but i mostly think it can be a tulpa. one thing i didn't say back there is that the times i saw it closer, the lights would start turning off and all the electronic equipment near it would just turn off. also any wireless device would lose the signal until it disappeared."

Another blog comment:
October 5, 2011 12:35 PM
Anonymous said...

"i'm not sure if this is relevant but in my dreams ALL of them i see a man wearing a top hat and a very dull purple robe, this man is unusually tall but not so much that he is obvious to me, any way, one night i remember falling asleep and seeing this man talking with a creature with spider like arms and wearing a hooded cloak...this was before i knew of the "slenderman" what say you?
p.s this man is not always obvious some times he is with me for short periods of time some times he is in the crowd. always with the same expression."

From October 2011:
"I have always been very scared of narrow things with long limbs, especially fingers. When something happens too fast for being natural, even video speed ups, i get a feeling that makes me terrified. I also remember something when i was 2 or 3, I don't remember if it was a dream or reality. I think that is the reason i am so scared about this stuff. What happened was that i waked up at night, and i saw something standing in my room. It was very tall with long arms, legs and fingers. I got

scared and dragged the cover over my head and hoped the thing would disappear. But instead, it scratched me through the cover. I don't know how long it did that, But then mom came into my room and the thing was gone. Maybe this was the Slender man"

October 28. 2011:

"my friend slept over one time and we stayed in the tent in the back yard. i had a history of sleep walking and talking so i thought nothing of this but my friend told me that during the night i rolled over and smacked her repeatedly, whispering "there's a man outside, there's a man outside" she was kind of used to my night ramblings by then but about two hours later i did it again giggling "the man is funny hahahaha so funny, go look" i never remember any of my sleep walking/talking escapades but my friend sure remembers this one"

Not an encounter, but an international connection from November 8, 2011:

"This is a very interesting subject which I encounter by accident while surfing the net. For your information I am from Malaysia in South East Asia and we also have entity similar to the Slenderman which is tall and has long stretched arms but we call it "The Bamboo Ghost" or in Malay language "Hantu Galah". Most probably because of the physical appearance of the entity itself. It is interesting to share this story because we might share the same entity but in different part of the world."

Another comment from November 21, 2011
 nate said...

"on october 20th 2011 i saw this man that fits all the descriptions of the slenderman i was driving in the woods and i saw a black figures about 20 yards from where i was. i stopped to get a better look at it and it was just standing there. I started to feel nervous so i pressed on the gas a a little and then his hands got very large and his fingers got as long as 3 feet! i floored it and i got out of the woods. it is November 21st and to this i have not seen him again. but every now and then i have a terrible feeling i am being watched some nights i cant sleep."

On February 2, 2012 Emma said...

"This might be my imagination but a couple nights ago when I and my three year old nephew were going to my late great grandmothers house to dry clothes I saw a figure matching slendermans I became worried for my nephew and told him to hold my hand until we got the clothes in the dryer drying and were back in the house I was so frighten by that figure that I stayed up the whole night with my nephew next to me my sister needless to say was worried when she saw me so exhausted I explained to her what I saw luckily she believed me because our family is religious people she thinks I may have seen a demon but after finding out about slenderman I am not so sure I'm scared about my sister and her kids living next to a wooded area with that creature lurking near by"

March 23, 2012:

"Very recently (before I had ever heard of the slenderman mythos) I had a dream of being outside on a dark night alone, when from down the road of the forested area I live in I noticed a bobbing lantern approaching. There seemed to be a procession of these terrifying shapeless slender creatures approaching, the first of which carried this lantern. They had elongated skinny limbs, and hunched posture. As they noticed me, they collectively rushed at me and attacked me. As they rushed at me, I noticed their limbs were not just skinny, but had odd protrusions and spikes and while I could make out their shapes, they were beyond black, they where impossibly dark in the way that I naturally associated them as shadows or demons. I told my brother and he mentioned the existence of this myth, and I found it striking how similar they are."

March 25, 2012:
"4 months ago i woke up form a nightmare and I swear I saw a tale thin man standing at the end of my bed i was so scared want under my blanket and cuddled my pillow then i looked and he was gone and now i feel like i was being watched"

March 29, 2012:
"I'll stay anonymous for this... So I remember from when I was young, I woke up in the middle of the

night. I looked towards the door as it was opened and I saw this strange figure... It was a simple entire head that would make a "be quiet" expression whenever it seemed as if I would scream. I did as it plead and eventually it came towards me... I can't remember the shape but I remember feeling at peace, like if a load came off my shoulders even do I was so young... I don't understand why or anything but I think it was slenderman. Nowadays I think of him all the time, infact I want to meet him and see if I can attempt at a conversation... Get a photo and set it up on facebook would be nice too."

April 10, 2012:
"When i was 7 i was reported missing for several days. i was found 15 miles away in a abandon house that was owned by my grandfather. When i was found i had no memory about what happened. i am now 18 i have my own apartment where i live with my boyfriend two nights ago i woke up standing in front of my window. i live on the second floor. There was a man standing there looking at me. i can remember what happened now

i was in my bed when i heard a knock at the window i went to the window and looked out i felt like i was just watching what i was doing i climbed out my window and walked away with him he asked me what i wanted most i told him i wanted my dad to quite hitting my mom i remember lots of colors and then i was taken back

two days later my dad did not come home from work i have not seen my dad since i was 7

ive seen the man a few times lately always when im alone always after dark im going to record my self sleeping tonight. i hope i can post proof!"

April 12, 2012:

"I believe he's real. I may be 13, and my eyes might be playing tricks on me, but I found out about him last monday morning. For the next two or three days I was terrified and couldn't even walk down the hallway by myself. I have been waking up early every morning- ranging from 2 to 5 am, sweating and feeling watched. I got up Saturday morning about 3 and watched tv in my living room in the dark. I kept looking out the windows, kind of hoping I would see him. Then I looked out one window and I saw a white-ish face with no eyes, nose, mouth or ears nearly pressed against the glass. I started freaking out but I couldn't move. I slowly turned on the lamp beside me and the face vanished. Again, this my just be my eyes since I haven't gotten much sleep, but I feel like he's watching me at night- waiting for me."

May 7, 2012:

I believe I have seen Slenderman. 2 friends (one girl, one guy) and I were headed to Seattle from San Diego and decided to make the long journey in one day. As we were entering into Northern California, it began to snow. The car we were in was old and a bit worn down. I was driving at that time as we were all rotating shifts in order to each get some sleep.

As the snow was falling I turned on the windshield wipers to make sure my vision wasn't hindered. As I mentioned before the car was old, so about 20 minutes in to turning the wipers on, they broke. We were all irritated by the inconvenience and had to stop at a gas station in the nearest town, Weed California.

We had our guy friend get out and make a phone call to his parents because we didn't know what to do. He had just joined the Coast Guard and was being stationed up there, hence the trip. We parked in a McDonald's parking lot facing a gas station directly across the street. As our friend was on the phone outside of the car, I looked up and instant terror shot through my body. I turned to my friend in the back seat who was sleeping and woke her... I needed someone else to see what I saw.

"Look out the window," I said, "can you please look at this man at the gas station across the street?" She looked up and had the same bone chilling reaction as me. She instantly rolled down her window and told our guy friend to get back in the car, that we needed to leave NOW.

The man walked eerily, hunched over with arms that seemed long enough to touch the ground. He had to have been 7-8ft tall, dragging something behind him. He turned the corner, never seeing us, or at least not caring that we were there. I had never thought to research anything about him, because I didn't know there was anything out there to find. After doing some research I believe he may not have looked over at us because he had no face...

We drove in to the gas station, stole a windshield cleaner and got back on the freeway as quickly as we could. We needed to get as far away from there as could FAST.

It's something I will never forget. Being a person who does not necessarily believe in this type of thing I can guarantee he was not of human origin. I don't know what it was, but the image of him will be burned in my my mind forever. I have never been so terrified by something in my entire life, I hope to never know that fear again."

May 8, 2012
"This is interesting. Won't go into detail, but a shadow in a fedora chasing ya around in your dreams is familiar....for me back in the mid 1970s.

All I can say to help is this...STOP FEEDING IT. Don't give it any reverence or fear. It has no strength without those things. Don't waste time on a path you're not meant to be on. I think most of us eventually tire of being afraid. Honest fearless prayer can help greatly. God Bless."

Specific Encounters

It stands to reason that some of the more recent encounters are more specific as to what the witnesses think they are encountering. So these encounters specifically fall into more detailed accounts of what we see in the Slenderman mythos.

August 16, 2011

"Me and 3 friends of mine have all seen the Slenderman, and none of us knew about the internet myth. my friend told me about something that he had seen at night about a week before i saw it, he described it as very tall and wearing a suit-like outfit, and asked me if i had any idea what it was. I had never heard of anything like it, and being curious i asked him to take me to where he had seen it. In my old neighborhood there was a hill of dirt where the construction workers dumped dirt from digging the foundations, and he saw it on top of there. the hill is surrounded by trees and about 50 ft from any roads. We started up the path and felt a chill so stopped and looked up at it, and saw a tall figure on top for a half second. the path up the hill is at least 100 - 150 ft. and a few seconds after seeing it on top we saw it again half way down the hill. the a moment after that it was at the bottom. the time it took to move that far was only a few seconds, and we all ran then. a few days later we saw it on the freeway and my friends freaked out and floored it, we were going 120mph and it was walking next to the car, not running but walking. We have seen it many times since then and still see it from time to time. and i would like to add that the hill we saw it on was covered in bushes that are about 5 ft tall, and the things body was more than halfway visible. even as im typing this i feel like its watching me, as i cannot stop shivering, and it is not cold in ohio this time of the year, and the last instance of this being recentley was that me and my friends were all sitting in my living room watching t.v. like normal. two friends decided to walk to the gas station to buy pop and we thought one had my other friends phone. we saw it in our backyard and attempted to call the frinds walking, as one had seen it previously, to tell them we had spotted it. the first call we made answered and all we heard was an odd staticy shriek. we called 6-7 more times all without answer. when my friend got home we asked him about it and he said the phone was in his room. we went to get it and it was under the bed."

October 27, 2011 ravenswood said...
"I used to see slender man when i was younger around nine or ten. i called him the octopus guy cause of his arms floating around. everyone just called me crazy and over time i forgot about it. but ever since my camping trip to big bear a couple months back when i saw IT again IT has been following me everywhere. stalking me observing me for only god knows why. ever since this all started for me again iv begun getting migraine headaches with nose bleeds, speech impediments, insomnia and iv been writing every occurrence on a

blog to keep track of everything. im still trying to figure out as much of this as i can and this helps out allot."

October 30, 2011 Keegan said...
"I would say that its a being or people that have been around, but it wasn't until he(them) were given a name that he(them) became widely known or acknowledged. so a tulpa, I suppose. Not that there was a specific point in time in which it was created, but that there have been (possibly multiple) point(s) of time where the mass consciousness has been reminded or made aware of the slenderman, followed by flare ups of activity concerning the slenderman. Whether or not the cause of more slenderman sightings is the attention of the public upon him, or that the cause of the attention is due to more slenderman sightings could be debated, but is irrelevant.

I personally had a run in with the slenderman, but until I discovered here in the past few days about him, I didn't have a name for him. He was merely the man in the woods. I had been out hiking with friends, and during the night several of the kids in my group had gotten sick. As the leader (sorta. the one that got stuff done) I had to run in between base camp and our outpost about a half a mile away several times starting at about 10:30 in the evening and kept on making trips back and forth with medics and taking items back t camp and the such until about 2 in the morning. During the trips back and forth I was mostly alone, and had the distinct impression of feeling watched, but couldn't see anything beyond some swaying branches and bushes (Camping in the pacific northwest). Finally, at around 2:30, I managed to crawl into my sleeping bag and fall asleep. However, I woke up half an hour later, needing to use the restroom. I woke up my friend who was in the same tent, and told him to just watch. I'm not sure why I did this. I think it was because I still felt off as though someone was out there. So I head out of the tent, go a couple feet away to take care of business. Anyways, while I was doing that, I suddenly got the chills, but looking around couldn't see anything but the trees again. I hurried up and headed back into the tent. My friend however asked me if I had seen the man standing beside me while I was out there, but he fell asleep before I could ask him anything more. The next day he went on to describe a man similar in appearance to the slenderman, but without the excess limbs. I knew that I had felt as though there had been someone there beside me, but had seen nothing. two days after it happened though, my friend couldn't remember what had happened at all, unless questioned thoroughly,at which point he would say he was getting creeped out thinking about it, and being visibly distressed wouldn't talk about it anymore."

November 25, 2011 Anonymous said...
"the slenderman is real I saw it we were alone as kids me and my friend he had just told me about it almost 5 minutes earlier, then as we were going back we heard walking across the street and like 6 feet away he was standing right there we ran back screaming... but my slendy didnt stretch his arms or anything he was tall and just walked toward us, since then he gets more pissed off and NOW he stretches although he did stretch before i got freaked out and looked it up"

February 28, 2012 Anonymous said...

"I am now 16 year old and I never heard of Slender Man until now, but what really freaks me out is that I had one of these dream experiences about the Slender man. I was 5 or 6 and I was having a dream of people I never knew or saw, playing a prank on me at a cemetary. There was one person up in a tree, recording everything, while I was walking. They buried a jack-in-a-box, so I couldn't see it, but when I did a hand came out of the box. The scary thing about the hand was it had long, unnatural, slender fingers that were trying to get a grib on my whole leg. It scared me, so much that I fought back and ran, searching my way out of the cemetary to the gates. Before I could reach the gates, I saw to my left was a moving shadow, I stopped before the gate to watch it, slowly moving to stand in front of me. When I looked up to see, the shadow had become a man wearing a suit, but he had no face, just a large grin. To me it looked like he had a cloak on, but on a second look they actually looked like arms. He tried reaching for me, but before he could, I woke up, screamed, then ran to my parents room. I never went to sleep in my own room after that, I

110

slept in my parents room for about 3 weeks, until I didn't have the dreams anymore. In those 3 weeks, I had that dream repeating over and over, and it would continue where it left off, showing me more of the suited man, but after he had a grip on me, I stopped having the dreams, but never forgot. Even now I have a feeling that i'm being watched and when I do, I automatically think about that dream. I don't know why, but I just do. Was that man the Slender Man the so called myths say? I only learned of the Slender man today from a friend, now i'm afraid if that man in my dreams was the Slender Man truely trying to get me or just loves to scare the hell out of people."

March 3, 2012 Anonymous said...
"Hello. I'm not so sure about whether or not this is relevant. But when I was young, around 8 or 9, I had an imaginary friend. The reason I say Imaginary is because my mother couldn't see him. Anyhow, this friend was tall. Really tall. I was five foot three at the time, and he was about three feet taller. He had four arms, and long spindly fingers. However, I did not ever consider the possibility of

him being Slenderman. Mainly due to the fact I did not know what slenderman was. Anyhow, he was nice, and friendly. I told my mother about him once, though. She got a look of fear and recognition. She told me the story of "The tall man". My mother is of German Descent, and she told me that The Tall Man was basically the bogeyman. He would wait until the adults weren't looking, then he would steal children away. I was frightened for awhile, but my friend...my IMAGINARY friend convinced me that he was nice. And that he didn't steal children away. He had a face...sort of. It was a strange face. the shape of it always changed. I cannot recall eyes or a mouth. However, I do remember him talking. He had such a smooth voice, even if he didn't have a mouth. Like I said, none of this may be relevant, for this man that I am talking about was probably no more than the imaginary friend of my childhood. However, I thought I saw him again. A couple weeks ago, outside my bedroom. I'm 18 years old, I had stopped believing in imaginary friends. I was starting to believe maybe he wasn't imaginary after all. I told my friends about the man, and they told me to look up slender man. And I did. Thus I am here right now. It is my belief that the person who won the contest for this internet "Hoax" Cheated. Because I believe I had met the Thin Man."

April 15, 2012 Anonymous said...
"I use to never believe in things like slender man....Till me and my friends became stupid and walked into the woods near a park which supposedly he has been well...seen. us being stupid wanted to see the truth....we grabbed flashlights and a couple cameras with night vision just in case.... once we got there it was about 3:00 pm But time flew by like never before! felt as tho it was an hour yet it was 9:00 PM. we found a circle with an X striked through it on a dead tree. at first we thought it was a joke. but then we began hearing a muffled laugh on our headfones then my friend DEAN dissappeared into the woods and we followed once we found him he was just standing there with somewhat gray eyes. he ran towards my friend Nick and yelled "Y DID YOU FOLLOW ME YOU SHOULDNT HAAAVE!!!!!!!" i thot he was playing till he began punching Nick. after we got him off nick he just fell to the ground and didnt

113

seem to remember it... about midnight we turned on the night vision and all. and we heard rustling leaves then Nick began screaming "Dude hes real hes real theres no face THERES NOTHING JUST NO FACE!"he pointed at wat he "saw" and wen we looked there was nothing yet he was still screaming "hes coming for me! hes trying to grab me!" he started to run then suddenly he flew off his feet to the side of a tree. we picked him up and on the tree was that same circle with an X through it. Then suddenly we all stared at the mark then looked up as we heard something and....there it was.... just standing there a black figure suit and tie. with a white musky face with no features. long arms and tendrils from his back. we asked "GO THE HELL AWAY! YOUR SCARING OUR FRIEND ILL CALL THE COPS!" then suddenly my ears rang with a screaming screeching noise i couldnt bare. i am 15 and on that day we sprinted out of the woods then i glanced back and noticed Nick was... gone. we ran back knives in our hands thinkin it was a person pranking us. saw nick bleeding from the arm with... that same circle carved in his flesh lightly. we woke him up and we just couldnt move...

something had Deans shoulder we could see black fingers on his arm so we slashed at them and before we noticed...they were gone. we took our chances and ran to the car and we all went home.... all the footage we took always had something wrng with it... ethier the audio wasnt working or there were odd loud noises we never heard.... nick still calls and tells us he wants to go back to the wood. and every time he asks we tell him if you go DONT YOU DARE COME BACK.... he hasnt gone since that day.... Wat happened???? im seeking ANSWERS"

On November 6, 2009 the paranormal and conspiracy themed Radio show "Coast to Coast AM" with host George Noory received many calls concerning Slenderman. Here is a partial transcript:

Caller 1: Have..have you ever heard of the Slenderman?
Noory: The 'Slenderman'?
Caller 1: Yes.
Noory: No I have not.

Caller 1: Well, the Slenderman is one of those uh, shadow people type stories that its common amongst kids and um, my girlfriend she told me recently that when she was younger, when she was a child, she got up one morning, she looks down the hall, and uh there is this man, the Slenderman. Um, and uh em…in the hallway. And he's described as having a um, he is very thin, and he wears a black suit.

Noory: Is he evil?

Caller 1: Uh, not sure, he…he, he's known as wanting to kidnap children, and I found this information on the Internet. And his uh, he has very long limbs, his arms stretch…

Noory: But he looks human.

Caller 1: He…he…he's humanoid, I'd say, he has sort of a Jack Skellington sort of look.

Noory: Um, uh, alright. I'll check out the Slenderman, I have not heard about him, uh, at all!

Caller 2: Um, I heard the caller talk about Slenderman?

Noory: The Slenderman, do you know anything about this thing?

Caller 2: Um, he's kind of been a big buzz on the Internet lately.

Noory: ok.

Caller 2: And there's these videos on Youtube uh, about these group of people who made videos and it appears to be seeing the Slenderman. Apparently he...he's stalking the..the director of the video? Um, and the Slenderman myth is that children, he appears to children, he comes and kidnaps children and children see him in their dreams.

Noory: Weird!

Caller 2: And he's very, he's very, very tall, almost like the last caller said like a Jack Skellington tree like tall.

Noory: Is this some kind of promotion you think, like a movie or something?

Caller 2: Um, I don't think so. Uh, um, it, its kind of zany, um, sometimes they will add videos and they'll show you know clips of these things. Weird things will happen with the camera or sound bytes. Um, he seems to have some sort of effect on the sound, the sound will distort whenever he is around.

Noory: Ok.

Caller 2: And the um, there has been uh, photos posted on the Internet from um, a library that burned in California?

Noory: Yes.

Caller 2: Um and in the picture there's a bunch of children and in the background you can see like almost a tall like figure. He's almost like a, like a Men in Black. He wears a tall suite, but he is faceless. And people are thinking that he's short of like a shape shifter because he is, he can extend his arms to great lengths and they can become like kind of like octopi type tentacles.

Noory: Is he hurting people?

Caller 2:They say that sometimes after he appears, children go missing.

Noory: Oh.

Caller 2: And sometimes they reappear and they have um, you know, a lot of trauma done to them that they can't recall.

Noory: But this is growing on the Internet, so it should be easy to find huh?

Caller 2: Yeah, yeah, it'll be easy to find, just type in the Slenderman.

Noory: Ok, we'll check that out, it could be a good story.

Caller 2: Yeah, yeah, pretty creepy.

Noory: Slenderman, Slenderman!

Caller 3: Hi George!

Noory: Hi!

Caller 3: I uh, I've been hearing people call in tonight talking about; I guess they call him "Slenderman"?

Noory: Yeah, what is this thing? Other than what people are telling me!

Caller 3: Well, um, first I wanna say that I feel very fortunate that as a person that called your show and got through then it is meant to be.

Norry: It is ment to be!

Caller 3: In '82, er '81 I gave birth to my son, um the following year my son um, I started having a lot of dreams. And um, I saw this thing in my dream, this what I believe is the Slenderman. And a very vivid dream, that was in '82 that I had the dream.

Noory: Ok. Does he look like what people are describing him to be?

Caller 3:He's skeletal kind of looking and yet human kind of looking, he's very long limbed.

Noory: Long limbed, long and gangly.

Caller 3: Um, gangly, but the thing is he was on Buffy the Vampire slayer movie series. I..I..had my son in '82. And you know how many years between that and Buffy the Vampire Slayer TV series. I saw this creature one night and I, I couldn't believe it. Then I researched it and there's a German folklore but they call it something to do with kinder, because it has to do with children. But I was very, very, um, then I knew there was, this thing was real.

Noory: So you don't think this is some Youtube hoax do you.

Caller 3: No. this is, uh, this is uh, the dark side communicating with humans. Uh, this um, you know, um, (sigh) I know from what I saw on Buffy, ok be…, from what I saw in my dream I am sitting in my dining room and this hobbled into the dining room and it's knees were level with its ears and , now on Buffy it hobbled into the chil..children's hospital. And it, to the, there are children there. And what, it did it stand up it was like, tall. And see what I saw in my dream it never stood up, and yet it hobbled in the room and I remember seeing things like up level with its head.

Noory: What's it want?

Caller 3: But it sounded like, when it moved its fingers, very long, it sounded like bamboo chimes you know like clinky clanky, almost like dry bones or something you would think of.

Noory: Like a skeleton.

Caller 3: Yea, but yet it had like skin but it had it looked like an old man in some way, it had long kind grey hair and long pointy features. But now Buffy is went a step further, because he opened his motuh and then he became more vicious looking.

Noory: Well, I tell you what we're gonna do, we're gonna have a show on Slenderman. Because this is the first I've heard about it and it is well worth looking into.

Email received January 15, 2010

"Pastor Swope,

I have been putting off writing this. I don't know if I am going crazy or seeing things. Things are really getting nuts right now. Let me start by saying that as a child I had many encounters with ghosts. I

121

think it started when I was about 3 or 4, I saw a man standing over my bed one night when I woke up. I don't remember being frightened. My mother told me it was my grandfather watching over me like a guardian angel. I remember seeing him every so often, but he did not have a face so I couldn't really tell if it was my grandfather or not (my mom had many family photos) My grandfather had died in what was to become my bedroom. Soon after the man watching me sleep incidents, I began to see spirits. They were not full bodied apparitions or anything, just wisps of cloudy stuff that had a vague human shape. Sometimes I would hear voices. When I turned 12 I stopped hearing he voices, but things in my room and sometimes around the house were out of place, like a spirit had moved them. Throughout this time I occasionally saw the man at the end of my bed. But when puberty hit, things changed. I had a creepy feeling about the man. He was normal sized when I was a cjild, but as I grew so did he. So I distinctly remember one night when I was 14, I woke up from my sleep and he was standing at my bed like usual, except he was HUGE. He was up to the ceiling and his arms were stretching out over my bed in a menacing way. He giggled like a little girl when I brought my covers up. I hit and called out for my mom and it was gone after she had come in and turned out the lights. After that it seemed like he wanted to get me. I would see him every now and then until adulthood. My mom passed away a few years ago, and the day after her funeral I was cleaning out her house. It must have been late in the afternoon. I was putting some sweaters in a box when I looked up and saw a shadowy reflection in the mirror. Behind me was the dark man and he was reaching out for me with 4 or 5 arms. I immediately screamed and turned around. Nothing was there. I left the house and only returned when others were with me. I swear though, every time I walked by a mirror even with people there, I thought I saw a fleeting shadow in the background. Since then I have not had eny encounters with the shadow man, until recently. This month has been hell. I just went through a divorce so I am sleeping alone again. I keep waking up, because I feel someone grabbing me. Two times in the last week I woke to see this giant figure arching over my bed like when I was a teenager, but like in the mirror, this thing had many arms. Once this week I woke up gasping for my breath like I had been choked. I couldn't breath, I can't tell you how frightening that is, and I have a sneaking suspicion that this dark demon is behind it.

So I am asking you, what should I do? Am I cursed? Is there anything you can do to help me? I am at my last straw, I have a nagging feeling that this thing wants me dead, and it will come to kill me soon. I do not want to go to sleep and I feel so frantic. Please help me!

Rita"

I tried contacting Rita via her email address through which she wrote me, but I have never received a reply.

Alien Encounters

Some of the oddest Slenderman like encounters fall in the realm Alien Abductions and encounters with odd beings after a UFO sighting. Here are two of these type that are the most alarming.

I met Stacie Bogart while working at a subsidiary of Hamot Hospital in early 2011. At the time I was compiling information about Slenderman and shared information about the Meme with her. After describing Slenderman Stacie had a look of shock. She had heard of this entity almost a decade before, but in the context of Alien Abduction.

Around 2002 Stacie had worked at another location and made friends with a woman who frequently had paranormal encounters. One of the most chilling was when in the middle 1990s when the middle of the might she woke up to see a tall dark and thin humanoid figure at the end of her bed. It reached out its arms and its finger elongated to an inhuman length and reached toward her head.

Stacie's friend was paralyzed, even though she tried to scream and move she could not. As the tendril fingers wrapped around her head she lost consciousness. The last thing she saw before loosing consciousness were the huge eyes in the creatures featureless face staring at her as if it was piercing into her very soul.

Soon after she noticed something was wrong, she was sluggish and drained. The world had become a dull and lifeless place; she was walking in a grey featureless world. She became ill, vomiting after meals for no real reason. Stacie's friend also began to experience frequent headaches that rendered her unable to cope with normal life. And sleep eluded her because of nightly nausea and dizziness every time she lay down in her bed.

Eventually Stacie's friend sought medical help, and as a consequence of her doctor's visit her physician ordered an X-Ray done of her head and upper torso. Mysteriously, the Doctors found a small metallic object had been implanted into the base of her skull. When the doctors tried to remove the foreign object they found that it had become entangled into the central nervous system at the spinal cord, and it was too risky to remove. The woman had never experienced any operation on her skull or nervous system; there was no record of where this object could have come from. The only solution was that this implant had been put in place during her frightening encounter with the dark man that horrible night.

When her friend had told Stacie this story, she was obviously skeptical. Even after showing her the scar on the base of her skull from the failed removal operation, it was a bit too much for Stacie to take. But feeling insulted her friend then brought copies of her X-rays to work and showed Stacie first hand that something was indeed implanted at the base of her skull that had become entangled into her spinal column that the physicians could not remove.

Perhaps this is one way that Slenderman can track his prey over their lifetime; through tracking implants.

After publishing this story on my blog article concerning Slenderman I received a letter on February 19th 2012 from a man named George.

"...The story of your co-worker's friend struck a real cord with me. I was never abducted, but I did see a UFO in June of 1996 near London, Ontario. It was a Thursday night and I was returning from work. I took a shortcut through a small rural road. It was a dirt road and really bumpy. Here was woods on either side of me on that road, and before I turned a corner, I saw a huge light rise from the woods to my right. It looked like a giant mushroom, as big as a football field hovering over the trees. I slowed down to look as I drove and then sped up to turn the corner so I might get a better view.

As I turned the corner I almost hit a really tall man wearing a suit who was standing in the middle of the road. I only saw him briefly, but he had to be over 7 foot tall with really thin and long arms and legs. The lights from the car shown right in his face, but the creepiest thing was I did not really see any features, only two big black eyes. I almost stopped, but this thing looked so unworldly and the UFO being there, I just took off down the road as fast as I could. I swear that thing followed me for a couple miles until I came to a main road. I didn't see the UFO after a while, but I swear I could see that man in the suit running behind me. I had chocked that up to paranoia but I swear that I saw the man in my house two times since then. I have written a UFO investigator, he said it might be men in black trying to scare me, but I swear this thing is not physical if you know what I mean. He is there one time and gone the next. After I read your Slenderman story I am afraid as all get out. It describes what I saw to a tee. How do I get rid of this thing?"

All these personal encounters show that something is up. Many of these incidents occurred and were narrated to me before the Slenderman mythos was created. What are we to make of this? Is Slenderman a real entity? Or is his archetype also shared with real entities that haunt the world? Let's take a closer look at entities, paranormal experiences in general and a few theories.

Of Phantasm and Fantasy

After reviewing the previous stories one is left with two simple options. The witnesses are either lying or telling the truth.

Of course the obvious option is to choose that the witnesses are lying. The Slenderman mythos depends on an active vibrant participation in order for the mythos to remain fresh and frightening. My conclusion that Slenderman is an actual entity would, of course, attract many of the ARG participants who would create imaginary stories to further the mythos. I have not included many emails and comments which I have received in this last chapter for that very reason. Most of those omitted stories were obvious fiction. Others, though, were more subtle, and it may be that some of the stories in the last chapter are fan fictions that are professed to be real encounters.

But, what if they *are* detailed eye witnesses of real encounters? Many of the stories occurred before the Slenderman mythos was created. Some of them were sent or related to me years before the mythos was started by Victor Surge. What shall we make of these?

When dealing with an eye witness encounter with the paranormal-especially supernatural entities- there are a few explanations (if you can eliminate fraud) that could explain the phenomenon.

1) The witness was hallucinating.
2) The witness mistook a normal occurrence for a paranormal occurrence.

3) The witness actually had a paranormal encounter with a supernatural entity.

Hallucinations are a common explanation by critics who attempt to rationalize paranormal phenomenon. Having a hallucination does not mean that the person has mental health problems or is on mind altering substances. Most of us have hallucinations at one time or another and really do not classify it as a "hallucination". Have you ever been walking down the street and see a person coming towards you and you either think the person is very attractive or very familiar? When the person comes closer, you see something totally different than you did when you were a far distance from the approaching individual. The distance blurred your perception and your brain filled in the missing pieces to make the image into something familiar or desirable. This is an optical illusion, and this type of hallucination is very common one.

Shadow creatures like Slenderman are a type of haunting that is commonly reported today. Many people see shadows move out of the corner of their eye. Sometimes these shadows are real, a slight change of light or a reflection from another object in the area. Periphery vision has very low resolution when compared to the center of gaze, called the fovea. Low resolution combined with decreased light gives an ample opportunity for the brain to fill in the gaps when an object quickly moves across our periphery in the dark. Many people who claim to have seen shadow people or creatures have seen them from their peripheral vision. This is extremely unreliable evidence for a paranormal encounter since there is a high probability of optical illusion in these situations.

Sometimes people see shadow beings head on, in the center of their gaze. Many times these creatures are seen as darker shadows in an already dim lit or darkened room. Once again the brain will fill in data that is not actually there. All of us have had visual illusions in the dead of night when we think we see things that are misrepresentations of what is really there. The sheets at the end of the bed are bunched up and look like an animal or a face. The stuff on the table looks like something unfamiliar and foreign. Many times minor illusions in dull light can be very vivid and lifelike. Perhaps many of these Slenderman reports are just simple optical illusions due to bad lighting and an overactive imagination.

But then there are many instances of people seeing shadow beings in clear luminosity or in the broad daylight. We will talk of those instances a little later in this chapter.

Many times people mistake a natural occurrence with a supernatural one.

It is different than an optical illusion, in that the person experiences the incident but consciously interprets it as something other than what it actually is.

In the paranormal field there are a lot of mistaken interpretations. All you have to do is view a few paranormal television shows and see that many of these shows show the teams making mistakes. But some mistaken interpretations are hard to catch, psychosomatic reactions are one example.

Psychosomatic reactions can be very dramatic given the right circumstances. Sometimes psychosomatic reactions can be as subtle as rapid heartbeat, loss of breath and unsubstantiated pain or as striking as welts, hives, swelling, rashes and in rare occasions a condition called *Psychogenic Purpura* where the body produces painful bleeding lesions, mostly on the extremities and/or the face. I have done consultation in many cases where a person thinks he or she might be demonically possessed and they possess physical scaring or blistering that the client sees as proof of demonic activity. Surely such a wound out of nowhere *has to be* supernatural, right?

Wrong.

The mind is an amazingly powerful thing. More times than naught the client has undiagnosed physiological issues or have been diagnosed and decided to stop taking their medication. Their hyper state of mind combined with possible uncontrollable supernatural elements victimizing them gives the right combination of elements for the body to respond to the person's psychosis. Even people that are highly suggestive can have dramatic psychosomatic reactions given the right conditions. The possibility or paranormal phenomena often is a trigger to these dramatic reactions in various people.

Psychosomatic reactions can be mistaken for paranormal activity.

Natural physics can also be mistaken for paranormal activity. One investigator saw a glass of water move across the table by itself. There was no object pushing against it via string or any other secondary force. Upon observation the investigator saw a thin film of water trailing the movement of the glass across the table. The water had a generous amount of ice and it had been a very hot day. There was an ample amount of condensation on the glass and the table was not quite level. Therefore the water falling down the outer side of the glass caused the glass to "hydroplane" down the table top. There is a plethora of unseen forces surrounding us every day that are natural and can cause things to move, drop from shelves or produce odd phenomenon.

Even intelligent, trained and detail focused individuals can be fooled by natural phenomenon from time to time.

With the Slenderman phenomenon, it well could be that people are actually seeing a tall man. He might actually be walking behind you. But it does not mean that he is paranormal. Or he could be just an optical illusion.

Lastly we come to the inevitable; the witness actually had a paranormal encounter with a supernatural entity.

Now this supposition itself might seem cut and dried. There is a Slenderman, he is an evil malevolent being that is going to hunt you down for the rest of your life until you are dead. But, that is not necessarily so. That is only one of three possible conclusions we can make if we are sure what the witnesses have experienced is an actual paranormal encounter. There are two other explanations.

First of these is that the entity encountered might be a mimicking spirit.

Demonology is not a science. There are hundreds of people who claim to be demonologists and have names for demons, origins of demons and histories of these diabolical entities. But all of this is mere conjecture. Names and histories are just associations, all an exorcist or demonologist can really do is make intellectual associations from the various phenomena and personalities that these malicious entities produce. It is a trial by error leaning experience. I myself am a Seminary trained exorcist and have been involved in pastoral counseling and helping people who think they are possessed for almost 30 years. I have learned that nothing is set in concreted. One of the most static things that you learn are there are types of demonic entities. One of them is the mimic demon. A mimic will pose as anything that will make you pay heed to it in order that it may further feed parasitically upon your emotions. The ones that can manifest physically are shape shifters; they can appear as Grandma or Uncle Ned or perhaps as a historical or mythical figure. They have been around for thousands of years and know humans better than any trained psychologist. They know personalities and prey upon people in order to feed on emotions and drag them down spiritually and mentally. They know what your reaction is going to be before you even do; they are not psychic, but devilishly smart and observant. Most of these entities thrive on fear. All of them want to destroy mankind and torment the individual. As observers of the human condition and history, they are aware of mankind in the modern era. They are aware of the Internet, they know of the Slenderman mythos. What a perfect persona to adopt if you wish to feed off fear!

So perhaps many who claim to be witnessing Slenderman are not really encountering him but a mimicking spirit. That is little comfort, since you are still confronted with a malevolent spirit that wishes you harm.

Secondly, you may be having an actual paranormal encounter with and entity that is of your own creation. Recently the paranormal field has been abuzz about a mystical concept of Tibetan Buddhism called a "Tulpa". A Tulpa is a literal creation of the mind by a trained or powerful magician, one Hindu book clarifies the nature of a Tulpa, "*In as much as the mind creates the world of appearances, it can create any particular object desired. The process consists of giving palpable being to a visualization, in very much the same manner as an architect gives concrete expression in three dimensions to his abstract concepts after first having given them expression in the two-dimensions of his blue-print. The Tibetans call the One Mind's concretized visualization the Khorva (Hkhorva), equivalent to the Sanskrit Sangsara; that of an incarnate deity, like the Dalai or Tashi Lama, they call a Tul-ku (Sprul-sku), and that of a magician a Tul-pa (Sprul-pa), meaning a magically produced illusion or creation. A master of yoga can dissolve a Tul-pa as readily as he can create it; and his own illusory human body, or Tul-ku, he can likewise dissolve, and thus outwit Death.[6]"*

The Tulpa in classic Tibetan Buddhism and modern witchcraft is a creature created through spiritual and mental intent by an adept practitioner of magic. The modern paranormal movement has adopted the Tulpa but modified how it manifests. The Tulpa in now recognized as a thoughtform that is manifest through the psychic energy of the witness or a third party. It is not a purposeful manifestation by volition on the part of the imaginer, rather it is an uncontrolled incidental manifestation of thought that becomes form.

However, a Tulpa is created by volition, not out of coincidence or random creation. So I feel calling an entity manifest out of the thoughts or psychic power of an individual needs another name. Therefore, I

---

[6] The Tibetan Book of the Great Liberation, Or, The Method of Realizing . By Walter Yeeling Evans-Wentz, Carl Gustav Jung, London, New York, Oxford University Press, 1954. p.29

141

advise that we call these though forms created unintentionally as a product of ***Parapsychodynamis***. Parapsychodynamis is the latent power to manifest paranormal phenomenon in various forms. Classic poltergeist activity that is usually focused around pubescent females has often been categorized as some sort of psychic manifestation due in part to the girl's pubescence. My theory is that the girl's latent ability is manifest through the hormonal changes and emotional anguish associated with puberty.

This theory postulates that all of us has various levels of Parapsychodynamis, that is, we all have a latent power within us that is made manifest though unconscious mental and emotional conditions.

When these powers become manifest we encounter a **Parapsychodynamic event** or a **Parapsychodynamic materialization**.

A pubescent girl who has poltergeist like activity (toys or objects moved around the house) is possibly unconsciously producing a Parapsychodynamic event.

And also many people who encounter ghosts, non-corporeal entities, legendary cryptids or UFOs are manifesting their latent power in a Parapsychodynamic materialization.

The Slenderman mythos is the perfect launching point for a Parapsychodynamic materialization. The mythos is incredibly creepy and paranoia driven. Your mind immediately races to the conclusions that would logically be raised if indeed Slenderman was real. And that psychic focus of emotional energy might produce an actual manifestation. Slenderman is actually formed out of the power of your mind. So in a very genuine way, Slenderman is indeed real.

Last of the three options is; we can come to the conclusion that Slenderman is real. The archetype of death that Slenderman embodies is not an archetype at all. Slenderman *is* the archetype. He is indeed death personified who from countless ages past has hunted down humanity with a relentless determination. If you see him as a child he will forever after haunt your dreams and your waking nightmares. The times you actually encounter his presence are the times that he is drawing near to take you to your grave. There is nothing that you can do about it, it is inevitable. Begging and screaming are useless; Slenderman makes no bargains and takes no bribes. Slenderman is coming for *you*.

How to Fight Slenderman

If indeed Slenderman is real either by Parapsychodynamic manifestation or as an eternal personification of death, then he poses an emotional and spiritual threat.

As someone who has had training and experience in dealing with paranormal encounters from a faith viewpoint, I can give some pointers on how to fight demonic entities including Slenderman. Of course as a Christian pastor, these pointers are based in the Judeo-Christian worldview.

Faith

When confronting malevolent entities, the best weapon you have at your disposal is faith. Christian Scripture tells us that Faith is, *"the substance of things hoped for, the evidence of things not seen."* Hebrews 11:1 (NKJV) While we cannot see God, we hope and trust. Since God is the creator and ruler of all creation, He has authority and power over any entity, spirit or demon. As children of God we have His authority in the spiritual realm. When confronting evil we must take this to heart. We must believe it. One of the principle weapons that malicious entities have is making you lose faith through fear and deception. You must keep your eyes focused on God, He is the one truly doing the fighting, you are His child and you are standing against this evil enemy is His name and through His authority, not your own. If you try to stand on your own, you will fail.

Prayer

Prayer is your connection to God, and thus the connection to your power source. Philippians 4:13 tells us, *"I can do all things through Christ who strengthens me."* (NKJV) God gives us power to fight the enemy; the confidence of faith, the determination to not give up, and the assurance of victory. While combating the demonic you will be tempted by lies. Lies that will attempt to make you give up. The best way to deflect these temptations is to keep in constant contact with God.

Commands

When confronting demonic entities such as Slenderman, commands need to be made. As a representative of Christ you have the authority through Christ to rebuke and command these entities to go away and bother you no more. They have no real power over you. With some entities it takes a repetition of commands because they like to believe they have some sort of stronghold in your life. They are claiming territory, either your dwelling or you, yourself. But you have authority, Jesus told His disciples, *"Jesus came and spoke to them, saying, "All authority has been given to Me in heaven and on earth."* Matthew 28:18. You have that authority as a child of God. Jesus is Lord of all spiritual beings, *"He (God) worked in Christ when He raised Him from the dead and seated Him at His right hand in the heavenly places, far above all principality and power and might and dominion, and every name that is named, not only in this age but also in that which is to come"* Ephesians 1:20-21 (NKJV)

Scripture

Lastly, you need to have the word of God. Satan and his demonic followers hate the Word of God because it documents the truth of their defeat.

For more on these steps and the commands, prayers, and scripture to use in combating demonic entities please refer to my previous work *"An Exorcist's Field Guide: to Blessings, Consecrations and the Banishment of Malevolent Entities"* available on Amazon.

A Few Last Words

I hope that you found this book informative and entertaining. It was my attempt to document what has been passed on to me. Something odd is happening. People are having actual encounters with malevolent entities that they claim to be Slenderman. If you have any other personal stories, feel free to stop by my blog and send me a message. I will leave you with an old Irish blessing:

May God grant you always...

A sunbeam to warm you,

A moonbeam to charm you,

A sheltering angel, so nothing can harm you.

Blessings,
Pastor Swope

Rev. Robin Swope is a Writer and has been a Christian Minister for more than 20 years in both Mainline and Evangelical Denominations. He holds a B.A. in Biblical Literature from Nyack College and an Masters of Divinity in Pastoral Ministry with an emphasis on Counseling from Alliance Theological Seminary. He has served as a short term Missionary to Burkina Faso, and has ministered to the homeless in New York City's Hell's Kitchen. He is currently the Pastor of St.Paul's United Church of Christ in Erie, Pennsylvania. He is also a freelance journalist for Examiner.com, and has also written for Fate Magazine. As a Seminary trained exorcist he has done consulting work with various paranormal investigators and television productions in the United States as well as investigators and writers across the globe